# PREACHING
# AND
# PASTORAL CARE

# SUCCESSFUL PASTORAL COUNSELING SERIES

# PREACHING
# AND
# PASTORAL CARE

ARTHUR L. TEIKMANIS

PRENTICE-HALL, INC., ENGLEWOOD CLIFFS, N.J.

Second Printing, July 1966

*Preaching and Pastoral Care*
by Arthur L. Teikmanis

Library of Congress Catalog Card Number: 64–23551

Printed in the United States of America. T 69511

PRENTICE-HALL INTERNATIONAL, INC., *London*
PRENTICE-HALL OF AUSTRALIA, PTY., LTD., *Sydney*
PRENTICE-HALL OF CANADA, LTD., *Toronto*
PRENTICE-HALL OF INDIA (PRIVATE), LTD., *New Delhi*
PRENTICE-HALL OF JAPAN, INC., *Tokyo*
PRENTICE-HALL DE MEXICO, S.A., *Mexico City*

Dedicated to
Vaughn Dean Dabney
and
Willard L. Sperry
who opened the door of preaching and
pastoral ministry to a delayed pilgrim
from the shores of the Amber Sea.

# INTRODUCTION

This series of books represents the most comprehensive publishing effort ever made in the field of pastoral care. These books could not have been published twenty-five years ago, or probably even ten, for the material was not then available. In the past, single books have been available covering different phases of the task. Now we are bringing the subjects together in a single series. Here we present a library of pastoral care covering the major topics and problems that most pastors will encounter in their ministry. Fortunately, not all of these problems need be faced every week or even every month. But, when they are, the minister wants help and he wants it immediately.

These books are prepared for the nonspecialized minister serving the local church, where he is the most accessible professional person in the community. It is a well-accepted fact that more people turn to clergy when in trouble than to all other professional people. Therefore, the pastor must not fail them.

*Russell L. Dicks*
*General Editor*

# CONTENTS

# PREFACE

PREFACE

When an invitation came my way to write on preaching and pastoral ministry, I responded with an ambiguity of feelings. Recognizing the invitation an honor and a privilege, I wanted to answer in a positive way. Yet, being fully aware that numerous books had already been written on related subjects pertaining to preaching and pastoral care, I hesitated. Looking at my own bookcase, I noticed more than a dozen volumes on preaching, pastoral calling, and counseling. My thoughts were: "Could I come up with something new? Could I illumine some unexplored areas in pastoral ministry? Could I disclose some resources totally unknown as yet?" Positive answers were not within my reach. The only originality I could claim would be my way of putting together pieces of mosaic, discovered a long time ago.

Then, in my mind, I turned to the idea of sharing. Upon reflection, I concluded that in several ways my ministry had been somewhat unusual. I was graduated from two seminaries—one on the continent of Europe, the other in America. By necessity, I had preached in four languages. In the depth of my soul, I had been sensitized by various apocalyptic experiences—by loss of home and country, by grief and separation, by sorrow, suffering, and human tragedy quite difficult to express in words. In the crises of life, I had been called to minister to those who were living under the shadows of the "Beast" as well as to the homeless refugees of World War II, weeping under the willow trees of a defeated "Babylon." After many years of struggle and adjustment, I had journeyed from fundamentalism to my own brand of Christian existentialism. By the grace of God, I had come to serve one of the finest churches of my denomination. Thus, without casting lots. I decided to share with others what I have found valuable and of

11

interest in my parish ministry, especially in reference to preaching and pastoral care.

As it will become apparent to any reader, the main emphasis in *Preaching and Pastoral Care* is on wholeness in our ministry. As preachers we need to be deeply concerned with the emotional needs of our people. At the same time, we must also remember their intellectual interests; their search for meaning, their need for communication, their will to understand. The social and the personal gospel belong together. In reality, they are inseparable—for, to know the redemptive love of God is to be concerned with the doing of justice and love in the society in which we live.

Preaching and pastoral care are as closely and dynamically related as love is to its expressions. It is by calling, counseling, and group participation that we discover what our people really need and whether or not we have been "truly called."

I submit this volume not as a startling discovery, but rather as a testimony that preaching and pastoral care are dynamically and inseparably bound together. In many ways preaching lives on the pastoral ministry. On the other hand, successful counseling depends upon dynamic preaching. Basically—and this goes for preaching to all sorts and conditions of men—preaching is pastoral care in the context of worship.

To my teachers at the University of Latvia, Latvian Baptist Theological Seminary, Andover Newton Theological School, and Harvard University I owe a debt of gratitude. Valuable insights gained from the members of my former parishes, my friends, and ministerial colleagues have been most helpful. I am indebted especially to Russell L. Dicks, without whose encouragement, help, and friendly guidance this book would never have been even contemplated.

My wife Austra and my daughters, Sylvia, Mahra, and Nora, have been a source of constant inspiration and help.

A final word of gratitude is due Mrs. Ethel P. Qualls and Mrs. Dorothy J. Johnson, secretaries of the First Congregational Church of Winter Park, Florida. Their assistance in the typing of the manuscript has been most valuable.

*Arthur L. Teikmanis*

## CHAPTER ONE

# MEANING And SIGNIFICANCE Of PREACHING

By wise and foolish men alike, preaching has often been held in contempt and disrespect. Recently, a theologian, lecturing on "The Arts and the Parish" made a statement to the effect that "in arts there is no room for preaching. When an artist begins to preach, he is through as an artist." No doubt, our theologian knew that good preaching is not didactic indoctrination any more than is good teaching, good poetry, and good art in general. He knew that preaching is not brainwashing. Yet, he evidently viewed some of it through the glasses of depreciation if not of despair. Only in private conversation did our scholar disclose that in his college days, and even before, he had suffered through much intolerably dull preaching.

At one time or another, all of us have probably heard an expression, "Don't you preach at me! I know what is right and what is wrong!" Inescapably, this implies an ignorant concept of preaching. It differs little from the labeling of all medicine as witchcraft, all psychiatry as shamanism, and the physical sciences as alchemy. No right-thinking person would indulge in such name calling. Yet, when it comes to preaching, there are so many who are prone to identify it with didactic moralizing or even with brainless pursuits to feed the hungry souls of men with nonsense unacceptable to men of intelligence.

## Not a Debased Form of Currency

It is hard to admit—yet, the truth remains—that all preachers have not lived up to their high and noble calling. Some have turned to preaching because of laziness; others, because of their own emotional instability. Some have chosen the ministry as an easy way to fame, power, and success; others have left the plow to enter the pulpit because of an eschatological illusion. Some preachers have been puritanical absolutists; others, liturgical escapists. Some have sacrificed at the altar of oratory anxiously awaiting the "glorious sound" of their own preachment; still others have turned their pulpits into limitless supply of emotional intoxicant. There are preachers who have exalted Jesus and have forsaken Christ crucified and risen; there are others who have wanted to know nothing but the day of his second advent. There are preachers who have taken care of their flocks as shepherds take care of their sheep.[1] There have been preachers who deserve no better title than one which Jesus gave to the false ministers of the gospel, "ravenous wolves in sheep's clothing."

For these and other reasons, preaching has often been held in contempt. Let us not, however, become defeated by our own anger and resentment directed against those who have spoken evil of preaching either because of their ignorance, arrogance, or professional prejudice. Let us remember the words of Jesus, "Blessed are those who are persecuted for righteousness' sake, for theirs is the kingdom of heaven" (Matt. 5:10, R.S.V.).*

Critics of the pulpit aim their darts at bad preachers who have exalted self above God; who have pre-empted His authority and proclaimed their own arrogance, ignorance, and vanity as infinite wisdom. The curses directed at preaching are really intended for preachers who have loved to be "seen in the pulpit" and have rejoiced in showman-like cliché prayers; who have rubbed salt in the wounds of those crying for healing ointment and have given stones to the worshipers asking for bread.

At the same time, as Franklin H. Littell has indicated, there are also historical reasons why "preachers have been reduced to the status of eunuchs" and preaching "regarded as debased form of currency, seldom treated seriously by men of letters and literary journals."[2] The popularity of religion in America has led many preachers first to eliminate the "offenses" of the gospel and then to present a "cheap grace."[3] As a result, all preaching has been in

---

* Scriptural references are from the Revised Standard Version, © 1946, 1952, by Division of Christian Education of the National Council of Churches of Christ in the United States of America.

disgrace. Very clearly, however, it is not preaching as such that needs to be thrown upon a scrap heap. We only need to be delivered from secular, unauthentic, and false preaching. True preaching is as indispensable as food and shelter and clothing, for no man can ever live by bread alone. Even more precious it is. As H. E. Fosdick has said in one of his prayers, "Deep beneath the needs which earthly things can satisfy is the hunger which Thou alone canst meet."[4]

The great Apostle Paul has affirmed the value of preaching another way: "But how are men to call upon him whom they have not believed? And how are they to believe in him of whom they have never heard? And how are they to hear without a preacher?" (Rom. 10:14).

If preaching were to cease, an unprecedented revolution would result which would affect not only the earth but also the sky and the planets. Parents would come to us and say, "You are taking away life's meaning and the faith of our children." Responsible citizens would complain, "You are undermining our morality, our social order, and our culture." Those hungering and thirsting after God's righteousness and love would pray so that the stones would begin to preach. Evidently, all preaching is not a debased form of currency. It is a necessary ingredient of genuine living.

### Religious Art Par Excellence

The truth stands; true preaching is religious art par excellence. To the extent to which it has to deal with the deepest feelings, attitudes, sentiments, hopes, and aspirations of human life, to the extent to which it calls for extraordinary sensitivity and thoughtfulness, intuition and empathy, imagination and realism, creativity and concern, it transcends all forms of secular—meaning shallow— art. Authentic preaching is never the art of oratory. It is not rooted in the preacher's ability to compose his sermons in scintillating phrases and poetic expressions. As Apostle Paul has indicated, even by "foolish preaching" men have been reclaimed from death and destruction (I Cor. 1:21, 2:4).

True preaching is not a stage production whereby a mask, an assumed personality (voice, expression), or a costume may enable the enchanted spectators to envisage what really is not there. The pulpit is not the place for showmanship. Authentic preaching is not an entertainment. It is not a solicitation of personal admiration, applause, or support. It is an art of mediation between God and man, between the needs of the soul and the reservoirs of spiritual supply.

Genuine preaching is religious art par excellence because it calls for creative and redemptive thinking, feeling, reasoning, and presupposing. It demands from every preacher an ability to blend the media of communication (direct and indirect) with the "truth of personality" in such a way that the eyes of the blind may see and the ears of the deaf may hearken, that the tongues of the stammerers may be able to speak plainly and the paralyzed may take their beds and walk. The art of preaching calls for creative abundance in such measure that by means of it the restless may be quieted and the complacent may be shocked, the sorrowing may be comforted and the comfortable be afflicted, that selfish egos may be crucified and buried and the sinners be raised from the dead.

"Brethren," said the former Dean of Princeton Theological Seminary, "your office and mine is to call men from the tomb. To make people alive. Alive at more points, alive at higher levels, alive in more interesting, worthy, and effective ways."[5]

## The Kerygma of God's Word to Men

C. H. Dodd's analysis of apostolic preaching is a profound one.[6] It is well documented and substantiated. Yet, genuine preaching is not at one time kerygma (proclamation), then didache (teaching), then homilia (discussion), then paraclesis (exhortation). No preacher can ever proclaim the good news of God without some interpretation, some discussion, some teaching, and some exhortation. In preaching, kerygma, didache, homilia, and paraclesis always belong together. Only the emphasis changes from time to time. What does not change is the kerygmatic form itself.

Paul R. Clifford has put it this way: "The important point is that kerygma should be the determinative of all that is said; fidelity to it is what makes a sermon real preaching. When this is grasped, didache and homilia are drawn into the service of human need, paraclesis in the way by which the congregation may be helped to make a genuine response . . ."[7] This is well said, for neither homilia nor didache nor even paraclesis can give to preaching its celebrative form of proclamation.

In a sense, authentic preaching is an "objective" proclamation. It is God's creative power we adore. It is God's truth we proclaim. It is God's redemptive love we glorify. It is the incarnation of God's spirit we celebrate. We are God's heralds, God's messengers, God's representatives. We are called to do His will and never "mix in" our own. Yet, we also need to remember "we have this treasure in earthen vessels."

From another point of view, genuine preaching is never merely an "objective" proclamation. We do not herald the news with an impersonal "heart and mind and soul." We do not speak with the "voice of God." We do always proclaim the Word as we have received, understood, and experienced. We do not proclaim the "old, old story"—something that God did so many years ago. Rather, through our preaching we are presenting the "story" that never grows old. Authentic preaching is a dynamic presentation of what God has done from the beginning, what he has done through the Man of Nazareth, our crucified and risen Lord, and what he is doing now. In such preaching, we are concerned with the meaning of his grace, truth, love, and the reality of our redemption today— rebellious, self-seeking, and estranged though we often are.

Authentic preaching is a celebration of God-given victory over the crises of life—be they the crises of sin and separation or the crises of failure, suffering, and loss. The victory is always from God, and any genuine victory is always a genuine celebration.

It is hard to understand how anyone could ever preach on that which he "knows not" and has not experienced. One can speak learnedly on matters beyond his experience; but, experience and encounter are the soul stuff of the sermon. Those who have experienced the grace that is all-sufficient, the truth that liberates, the power of resurrection in death and the power of overcoming, are best equipped to proclaim them with enthusiasm, conviction, and rejoicing.

Authentic preaching is meaningful presentation of that which "is and was and ever shall be." Dean Roy Pearson has put it eloquently and dynamically:". . . there must be no contentment in the parroting of hallowed phraseology. One neither speaks to Spaniards in English nor whispers in Boston when he wants to be heard in London. The gospel according to Matthew and Luke must be preached in terms of Oak Ridge and Las Vegas."[8]

## Contemporary Extension of Incarnation

True preaching is not only speaking the truth; it is also "doing the truth." It is our participation in the redemptive drama of God. True preaching is contemporary incarnation of the Eternal Word. As Donald G. Miller has put it, "To preach is not merely to stand in a pulpit and speak, no matter how eloquently and effectively, nor even to set forth a theology, no matter how clearly it is stated or how worthy the theology. To preach is to become a part of a dynamic event wherein the living, redeeming God reproduces his act of redemption in a living encounter with men through the preacher."[9]

True preaching is an act of redemption whereby as preachers we are called to have partnership with God and proclaim in his name the primordial words spoken against the darkness of a thousand midnights, "Let there be light!" (Gen. 1:3). In the name of God, we are commissioned to preach with a flaming conscience and an awareness "the Spirit of the Lord God is upon me, because the Lord has anointed me to bring good tidings to the afflicted; he has sent me to bind up the brokenhearted, to proclaim liberty to the captives, and the opening of the prison to those who are bound; to proclaim the year of the Lord's favor, and the day of vengeance of our God; to comfort all who mourn; to grant to those who mourn in Zion—to give them a garland instead of ashes, the oil of gladness instead of mourning, the mantle of praise instead of a faint spirit; that they may be called oaks of righteousness, the planting of the Lord, that he may be glorified" (Isaiah 61:1–4). As participants in the redemptive drama we are charged with the responsibility to proclaim in the spirit of Christ:

Your sins are forgiven! (Luke 7:48).

Rise up, take thy bed and walk! (John 5:8).

Fear not for I am with you, be not dismayed, for I am your God; I will strengthen you, I will help you, I will uphold you with my victorious right hand (Isaiah 41:10).

Be still, and know that I am God (Psalm 46:10).

You are the salt of the earth (Matt. 5:13).

You are the light of the world (Matt. 5:14).

Go therefore and make disciples of all nations (Matt. 28:19).

When a preacher is aware of his glorious calling, he is then destined and bound to become a channel, a mediator, a manifestation of the truth, the love, and the power of God.

## Pastoral Care in Worship

Dynamic preaching is basically pastoral care in the context of worship. The preacher who has done his pastoral work diligently knows that his congregation is not a fellowship of saints. They are sinners called to be saints of God. They are people troubled about many things. The preacher who has been around in his parish knows that most people do not wear their hearts on their sleeves. Some people laugh to conceal their tears. Others boast to hide their inferiorities; still others behave aggressively because they are basically insecure. The preacher is fully aware that there are members in his congregation who have come to the service of worship with a sense of guilt, anger, frustration, loneliness, and despair, while others have come with inquiring and growing minds and are concerned with the problems of life, of culture, and human existence.

Many times I have sat at my desk thinking about the people of my former parishes. I remember so many of them. There was a wealthy man to whom a physician had said, "It is spinal arthritis. (It really was spinal cancer.) All I can do for you is to give some aspirin." The man came to me and in great disappointment said, "Think of it, I will have to take twelve tablets of aspirin every day for the rest of my life. Well, probably I will have to swallow a million tablets in my lifetime." There was a wonderful worker for all good causes who was left emotionally stranded by her unfaithful husband. There was a war veteran who was living in constant anxiety and fear. I could never forget a young elementary school teacher fighting desperately with her problem of lesbianism. There was a man who felt guilty and frustrated because he had flunked out of a medical school. With deep empathy I am thinking about the countless tears of a young couple shed over their retarded little daughter. There was a scientist who tried to drown his problems in alcohol and his wife who lived on the verge of a breakdown. There were people who were "marked" by their hospitalization in a mental institution and others who needed such help but would not avail themselves of medical treatment. There were men and women who had been spiritually and physically injured and others who had not yet been awakened to maturity. There were people alert, responsible, eager to serve, while others were there who lived on the love and sweat and tears of others. There were intellectuals who were pitifully unbalanced and emotionalists who lived in the world of illusions. Some members of the congregation were smug, complacent, and given to gossip, while others there were with overactive superego. Without words, I could hear them speak, one after the other: "Preacher, do you understand my problem? Is there any love and empathy in your heart? Are there any spiritual resources that could renew my life? Preacher, if you are a man of God, speak to me of his love and grace and truth that I may know them and live."

As James W. Clark has put it, "All preaching is preaching to personal needs, if it is really preaching and not the delivery of an essay or a general address to nobody in particular or mere vocal muscle flexing. It is the transmission of God's truth through a person to a person."[10] Speaking about the secret of Dr. Fosdick's effective preaching, Mr. John D. Rockefeller, Jr., is reported to have said, "The greatness of his preaching lies in the fact that each person in the congregation thinks he is preaching to him. I never hear him but I say, 'How does he know my problem?' "[11]

"A Questionnaire, seeking answers at this level, queried the man in the pew," says Edgar N. Jackson. "The purpose was to find out what people want from their pastors through their sermons. About half of the 4,000 queried indicated a concern about intensely personal matters, such as the futility of life, insecurity in personal relations, a haunting sense of loneliness, problems that involve marriage and the proper control of the sex drives, the effect of alcohol, false ideas of religion and morals, a feeling of inferiority, the problem of suffering as well as the problem of illness, and the feeling of guilt and frustration. Another fourth of those who responded were concerned about family problems, parenthood and childhood training, infidelity, religious differences, and other problems that were symptoms of tensions in human relations. The remainder and relatively small minority were concerned about social, community, and more traditional religious problems."[12]

True preaching is not a generalization nor is it a monologue; it is always directed to the needs of the worshipers. At the same time, passive, non-participating listening to a sermon is not a true worship. The goal of true preaching is to elicit an active participation of the worshipers in the pew. Says Gene Bartlett, "If preaching is a real person-to-person engagement, then the listener is far from passive, but indeed has his own active part to play . . . When preaching becomes real, here as at few points the listener lays open the center of his life for reexamination and exposure. Here in a seeming privacy and anonymity of the pew, a person weighs the great questions of his life, the value he is seeking, the moral decisions he is facing or evading, the basic reliances by which he is living, the direction and destiny of the years."[13]

When preaching is directed to personal needs, worshipers in the congregation respond, sometimes with smiles and then again with tears, sometimes with excitement and then again with deep reverence, sometimes with quiet thoughtfulness and then again with a challenging disturbance. The preacher who is also a pastor is bound to notice such reactions and respond to them without a red-pencil mark in his manuscript. Such creative and redemptive experience in the service of worship is mediated only by the preacher who knows his people and their needs, whose heart is filled with empathy, love, and understanding, who knows the true meaning and significance of preaching.

**CHAPTER TWO**

# WHOLENESS In Our MINISTRY

It is very true that "a home-going parson means a church-going people." Yet, the phrase is quite misleading. Pastoral care is not a means to another end—it is an end itself. It is an indispensable part of our Christian ministry. As Paul R. Clifford has said, "The idea of a pastoral call being an end in itself cannot be too strongly emphasized. Only when it is seen to have a definite end inherent and objective as the visit of the doctor or the social worker will it be delivered from the embarrassment that has so often characterized it."[1]

## We Call with a Purpose

At one time or another, probably, all of us have felt that pastoral calling is an unimportant function of the Christian ministry. For one reason or another, even a parishioner may have suggested, "You should not have troubled yourself calling on me." Some time ago, a young seminarian complained, "What do you do when you call on a person that says, 'Don't bother calling on me. You have other things to do! Don't waste your time.'" The first answer that comes to my mind is this: "Don't make a mistake! Everyone wants to be noticed and appreciated. Behind the words, 'Don't waste your time on me,' may be totally different thoughts. The parishioner may be saying, 'Preacher, do you really care? You are just a young preacher. Do you understand what the problems of life are? I am not going to open my soul to you until I am absolutely sure of your true intents and purposes.'" In such a situation it is well to say, "Now what makes you say that?" or, "What do you mean by saying, 'Don't waste your time on me'?" or, "What do you think are the real responsibilities of a pastor?"

22

We do not call primarily to find illustrations for our sermons, nor should our motivation ever be to fill our churches with personal admirers. We do not call simply to raise our budget or to cement our church organization, although this, too, needs to be done. Yet, these are not our primary purposes in calling. We call to find out who our parishioners are, where they have come from, what their family and religious background is, and what their problems are. We call to establish a rapport, to build a bridge of friendship, to manifest our interest, love, and care.

World War II was almost over. The Third Army had already reached the city of Munich, Germany. I am sure, at this time, the American chaplains were more busy than ever. Yet, as soon as they learned about the liberated strangers in the city of Augsburg, they came to see us. One after another, they assured us of their love and concern. They kept on asking, "How are you making out? What can we do to help you?" Even before they did anything else, their friendship, their interest, and their concern constituted for all of us the gift of beauty for ashes, the oil of joy for mourning, the garment of praise for the spirit of heaviness.

### Parishioners Expect Our Calling

We call because our parishioners expect us to remember them. When we fail to do this, most of them feel neglected—even despised and rejected. There is a family in my present parish on which I had failed to call within the first four months after my arrival in Winter Park. When the time of our every-member enlistment came, the secret was disclosed. Our "forgotten" family felt hurt. They told the enlistees, "The preacher has not been around. Most likely he doesn't care for us old people." Without delay, I visited this family. I told them that there were many others I had not managed to call on as yet. For a few moments, our relationship was icy and distant; yet, soon a rapport was established. Only moments after the ice was broken, one of the members of the family said, "We want you and your wife to come for dinner. We have always done this for our ministers. We hope you will find it possible to accept this our invitation." Here was a partially shut-in family that needed the minister more than medicine and physicians' care. Needless to say, their annual pledge to support the program of the church came in with the next mail.

To many of the shut-in members of our parishes, pastoral calling is one of the most significant events of their lives. Not long ago I made a special effort to visit a shut-in member of one of my former parishes. This person is confined to bed in a large nursing home in the North. Obviously, her memory is fast failing. She remembers faces but not names. As I entered her room, I called her by name, kissed her on the forehead, and said, "This is your former minister," and gave my name. "I came to see how you are doing and to tell you how much you have been in our hearts, especially during these six months of your illness." The patient recognized me, smiled, and said, "Oh, how good, you have come to see me." Her speech was only partly coherent; yet, it was evident that my visit had filled her day with joy. Later on, her daughter said, "Mother was talking about your visit throughout the whole week. To her, this was the happiest experience of the six months' confinement in a nursing home."

As someone has said, let us make no mistake about it—pastoral calling is never merely a personal friendship call. Ministers are God's ambassadors who speak for him and the church. Even when nothing "specifically religious" happens in our visit, we have brought about an inspiring, stabilizing, and uplifting influence in the lives of our people.

## Moved by the Love of Christ

Pastoral calling is evangelism in reality. It is evangelism par excellence because it is carried on in a person-to-person relationship. This kind of evangelism has been praised in the gospels as a *sine qua non* of Christian discipleship. Unmistakable are the words of Jesus: "Depart from me, you cursed, into the eternal fire prepared for the devil and his angels; for I was hungry and you gave me no food, I was thirsty and you gave me no drink, I was a stranger and you did not welcome me, naked and you did not clothe me, sick and in prison and you did not visit me" (Matt. 25:41–43). We call because we ourselves respond to the grace and the truth proclaimed through our preaching.

We call to assist our parishioners to become reconciled with God, to make adjustment to life, to choose in freedom and responsibility, to grow in Christian maturity and other-love. When, however, we find it difficult to do this or when we think that calling is a waste of time, the moment for self-examination is at hand.

Not long ago a disillusioned minister came to tell me that he had decided to leave the ministry. In response to my question, "Why?" he gave a multitude of answers. He told me how much he liked to preach but did not like to call. He said, "You know, my parishioners are so terribly hostile—they are full of guilt and frustration. I cannot manage to make a pastoral call." I said, "Are you saying that you still love your people, that you know what to do when they are guilty, frustrated, and hostile but you are afraid of their hostility? Are you saying you have no trouble facing friendly parishioners?" At this time, tears appeared in his eyes. He said, "I know it is my own guilt, frustration, and hostility. These have blocked the way. But how do I overcome them? How do I establish a positive relationship?" I repeated one of his questions: "How do we ever . . ." He interrupted me and said, "Have you ever experienced anything like this? Do you really know how I feel?"

After a two-hour, soul-to-soul searching and sharing, my visiting friend exclaimed, "For the first time in my life, yes, for the first time in my life I feel I am accepted by another minister. I know, with the love of God in my heart, I will be able to face my people."

## Ready to Render Assistance in Crises of Life

We call to render service to our people in their moments of crises, whether the strain in relationship be between husband and wife, parent and child, friend and friend, employee and employer, or between different races, creeds, and nationalities. To use an expression of Cabot and Dicks, "We call to render service to our people at the point of their growing edge."[2]

In every parish there are men and women who live in isolation and despair. They need our visitation. There are husbands and wives who have grown apart and are a burden to each other. They need our counseling. There are parents desperately worried about their rebellious children. They need the assurance that such a rebellion if carried on in the open is normal, healthy, and natural. There are people, both young and old, who are fearful and guilty and hostile and are in need of someone to listen, to love, and to lift. Their crises of life are our opportunities to render service and help.

Visitation opens the door of opportunity to people to vent their feelings—whether they be guilt, frustration, or hostility. A preacher who has done his calling knows that such feelings are quite universal and they are dynamically interrelated—guilt leads to frustration and frustration to hostility. Says Paul Tillich, "Have you ever noticed how much hostility against God dwells in the depths of the good and honest people, in those who excel in works of charity, in piety, and religious zeal? This cannot be otherwise; for one is hostile (consciously or unconsciously) toward those by whom one feels rejected. Everybody is in this predicament, whether he calls that which rejects him 'God,' or 'nature,' or 'destiny,' or 'social condition.' Everybody carries a hostility toward the existence into which he has been thrown, toward the hidden powers which determine his life and that of the universe, toward that which makes him guilty and that threatens him with destruction because he has become guilty."[3]

Grief-stricken members are to be found in all of our parishes. Some of them are hurt by their loss of health, status, ability or professional prominence. Others are distressed by the loss of a loved one. All need a friend. They need a minister. Here is a pastoral opportunity to render a manifold service. These people are in need of somone to listen to their woes and heartaches, someone to help them establish new relationships and discover new pathways to meaningful existence.

## We Call in Every Emergency

Death in the family is an emergency which calls for an immediate response by the pastor. After having witnessed many a situation of this kind, for his own protection a minister may be tempted to develop a cold, professional attitude. This a true pastor cannot afford to do. He must be calm, yet sympathetic. He must be hopeful, yet realistic. He must be ready to listen, yet also to speak words of comfort and consolation.

As William Rogers has pointed out in the September (1963)

issue of *Pastoral Psychology*, the grief-stricken individual has many needs. He needs, first of all, someone to support him emotionally. There is also a need to express one's sorrow, to actualize one's loss. There is also a need to verbalize one's feelings of guilt and verbalize one's feelings of hostility. Blessed is the pastor who keeps these needs in mind as he calls upon a grief-stricken family. And, blessed is the pastor who has words of comfort and encouragement: "Underneath are the everlasting arms"; "God is a very present help; he is present now to give you strength"; "We have this confidence that nothing can separate us from the love of God."

It is equally important that we call immediately following an accident. A young man had just been injured in a motorcycle mishap. Both parents were desperately concerned. It looked as if the boy were going to have a permanent brain injury. The parents called our church office and asked me to pray. I assured the frightened father and mother that I shared their sorrows and hoped that all things would work out for the best. Without a loss of time, I visited the young man who was already improving. Later on, when it was evident that the boy would have no permanent injury, I received a letter of gratitude. There was tumultuous rejoicing. I am almost certain that nothing could break the rapport between this family, the church, and the preacher.

Sickness and hospitalization are on my list of emergency calls. As far as possible, I make an effort to visit all hospitals in our area at least twice each week. Nevertheless, when a telephone rings and the message is about a parishioner just admitted, I try to free myself as quickly as possible to visit such a person. Here is a real opportunity to serve. My procedure in hospital calls is a simple one. First, I try to establish a friendly relationship. Then, I encourage the patient to speak about the things that seem to matter most. Directly or indirectly, I try to assure a suffering person of God's healing power, his love and care and his presence. I always offer a prayer. Only twice have I been told not to pray. In both instances, however, when I began to leave the room, the patients called me back and asked me to offer a prayer. Here is one of my prayers for the sick:

Our Father God, who art the source of healing and strength, behold us as we come to thee in this hour of need. We know, in thee we live and move and have our life. We know, thou art beneath us to uphold us, above to uplift us, around to protect us, and within to give us strength. We are sure, underneath are thy everlasting arms. We only pray thee, O God, to make us constantly aware of thy presence, thy healing power, thy love, and thy care.

Thou art gracious, God, and merciful. With thee is forgiveness, courage and hope. We accept these as thy gifts of grace. With thee is sufficient strength for our every need. We accept this strength—physical and spiritual—with gratitude and thanksgiving.

Help us always, O God, to remember thy promises to us. Enable us so to co-operate with thee that fears, doubts, and anxious cares may vanish from us, and quietness, confidence, and trust may fill our innermost being. Even the deep feelings that we do not know how to express in words we bring before thee and ask that in all things thy will be done. Hear us, we humbly beseech thee. Amen.

When a telephone rings and a voice on the other end says, "Pastor, I guess I will not be able to bear this strain any longer; something dreadful is happening to me; I am frightened; please, come as soon as you can," I respond immediately. Without ever assuming the role of a psychologist, much less that of a psychiatrist, we can render important service to our people at such times of great distress. At times, this kind of visitation and calling may be costly indeed. Yet, woe to the minister whose ears are deaf to the calls of emotionally distressed parishioners.

## An Inseparable Relationship

Pastoral calling is never to be viewed as an appendix to the ministry. Through calling we learn about the specific needs of our people. Through calling we establish a rapport for preaching and counseling. Through calling we assure, encourage, inspire, guide, and direct our people. Through calling we bring about an uplifting and stabilizing influence. Through calling we encourage our people to do likewise in our churches. We may do well to ponder the words of Phillips Brooks, "You may easily come to believe that it would be good indeed if you could be one or the other of two things, and not both: either a preacher or a pastor, but not the two together. But I assure you, you are wrong. The two things are not two, but, one . . . The preacher who is not a pastor grows remote.

The pastor who is not a preacher grows petty . . . Be both; for you cannot really be one unless you are also the other."[4]

As we have seen, pastoral calling inevitably leads to counseling at home, in the hospital, and in the nursing home as well. At the same time, true pastoral care demands that counseling be done also in the pastor's study. In respect to this kind of counseling, some preachers have advanced numerous objections. The first of these complaints has to do with what some preachers have regarded as a fundamental functional difference between preaching and counseling. Some maintain that a preacher must fearlessly proclaim the gospel regardless of "where the chips may fall." Preaching, it is said, deals with oughtness, judgment and exhortation. The truth must be proclaimed regardless of how it may hurt. Good counseling, on the contrary, requires the counselor to abstain from condemnatory judgment, objective proclamation and exhortation. Consequently, a question is advanced: "How can one person fulfill two functionally different tasks?"

Seward Hiltner has answered such queries well by pointing out that "the trouble with this question is not in what it says about pastoral counseling, but in what it implies about preaching . . . True preaching cannot possibly say anything to the congregation that is not also said to oneself.[5]

The *oughtness* of the gospel is proclaimed by convictions rather than condemnatory judgments, by indicatives rather than cold imperatives, by admiration and wonderment rather than compelling exaltations. At this point we only need to remember the parables of Jesus to see how "the ought of responsive action arises not out of exhortation, but out of conviction that both things are as they are— man's lostness, and God's salvation."[6] In counseling also, our aim is to help an individual to see things as they are—our lostness and God's salvation. Clearly, the difference between counseling and preaching is not a fundamental one. In both, the aim is the same.

Another objection some preachers have advanced against counseling may be formulated in this way: "I cannot advertise my counseling hours as do other professional men. People do not know that I am ready and willing to help. They do not come."

This is only partially true. Of course, in good taste, we cannot hang out a shingle in front of our church office saying, "Pastoral

Counseling from 10:00 A.M. to 12:00 A.M." There are effective ways to make known our willingness to render counseling services. One of these is by the type of preaching that evidences our love for people, our respect for their otherness, our understanding of their problems, predicaments and emotions, our insight into the dynamics of personality (with all the intricacies of ego defenses), our sincerity, and our confidence in the love of God. To be effective in counseling as well as in preaching, one needs genuinely to love his people. Without such love, all tools and techniques are of no real value. In both—counseling and preaching—one needs to understand that the best one can do is mediate God's grace, his truth, and his love. Whether in counseling or in preaching, one needs to realize that the destructiveness of our negative and ambiguous feelings is overcome by our acceptance and understanding of such feelings. Through this acceptance they are released from their demonic powers. In both—counseling and preaching—one needs to be able to respect the otherness of the other without being judgmental and condemnatory.

What our people want to know is whether or not we are really concerned with their needs, whether or not we are the same in life as in the pulpit, in counseling as in the sacrament of the Holy Communion, the same in listening to their problems as we are in listening to their joys. Our people want to know whether or not we are truly willing and competent to render such counseling services as they need. This we can make known through everything we say and do in the pulpit as well as in our home visitation. As Edgar Jackson has put it, "Through his program of pastoral calling, hospital visitation, and person-centered activities, he indicates his interest of the people in the parish . . . The clergy is still the one soul healer who seeks the total person—mind, body, and spirit; instincts, emotions, and reason."[7]

It is by his attitudes toward his people, whether in pulpit, in home visitations or in fellowship projects, that a preacher establishes his reputation as a man worthy of confidence and trust. When the parishioners know that their preachers care, they do not hesitate to come even though they may say as they enter, "Sorry to take time from your busy schedule." Again, we must emphasize, preaching and pastoral work are inseparably bound together.

We know that in the office of pastoral counseling, there is no room for moralizing, however much we like to call this "prophetic ministry." A person who is already brokenhearted needs not to be broken more. An individual who is already guilty needs not to be shocked and shamed into more guilt and condemned into despair. A parishioner who is already suffering from the consequences of sin needs not to be told how terrible and costly is his disobedience to God. Jesus did not condemn anyone who came to him in humility and repentance. Neither is there any room for self-righteous moralizing, criticizing, condemning or denouncing in our counseling or our services of worship.

## Insights Gained Through Calling

It is through pastoral calling and counseling that the preacher gains valuable insights into the innermost lives of his people. He learns to know what questions they ask, what they are thinking about political, racial, and cultural problems. He discovers their hopes and fears and aspirations. He becomes acquainted with their religious orientation, their thoughts about God and Christ and eternal life; about sin, judgment, and retribution; about suffering, love and atonement.

Visiting an elderly lady in my parish, I learned something I thought people had asked their ministers a century ago rather than today. Under the pressure of grief, this woman turned to me and said, "Can you tell me where is heaven and where is hell? What is your concept about the events of the final judgment? Where will it take place?"

It is through our pastoral ministry that we learn about the manifold crises of life—the crises of failure, grief, loss of self-esteem, physical sickness, and dying.

A tearful young woman came to my study and confessed a sense of guilt that had haunted her for many years. She began by saying, "We have done it all wrong, and I feel terribly guilty." After a prolonged search, we discovered that at the age of ten she had told an untruth to her teacher. This had happened on a ball field. In order to get a lollipop, she had told her teacher that it had been an honest-to-goodness home run, although she had been aware that she didn't touch third base. She had buried the guilty feeling deep within herself and had shared it with no one. Judging from her smiles and her laughter, it would have been hard for anyone to have predicted that there was a deeply buried feeling of guilt in her soul. As a preacher, I learned it only after a prolonged personal confrontation and discussion.

It is through our pastoral ministry that we come in direct contact with anxiety and grief, loneliness and despair, impulsiveness and instability, immaturity and insecurity.

After a third visit to my office, a man told me that for the past ten years he had lived in a licentious promiscuity. He confessed that besides his wife he had had numerous "sweethearts." Never had he been able to choose one. He had lived for these many years as a victim of desperate insecurity, guilt, and confusion.

It is through our calling and counseling that we become acquainted with our parishioners—the oversensitive and suspicious, the irresponsible and the rebellious, the proud and the arrogant, as well as those questing for deeper knowledge, love, and understanding.

The words of Eliza Doolittle in Bernard Shaw's *Pygmalion* may well apply in a situation of a preacher who wants to do his preaching yet despises his pastoral ministry, "Don't talk of love—show me!" Our ministry is never complete if it is a ministry on Sunday morning only, however inspiring and helpful that may be. If there is to be a healthy wholeness in our churches and in our ministry and within us as preachers, we need to find a way to integrate our words with our deeds, our preaching with pastoral calling and counseling.

## CHAPTER THREE

# READY For GENUINE PREACHING

## The Principles of Group Dynamics

Since preaching has to do with the worshiping community as a group, it is necessary that we as preachers acquaint ourselves with the basic principles of group dynamics. Sigmund Freud's *Group Psychology and the Analysis of the Ego* may provide some valuable leads.

Here is one of Freud's theses about group behavior: "Groups have never thirsted after truth. They demand illusions, and cannot do without them. They constantly give what is unreal precedence over what is real. They are almost as strongly influenced by what is untrue as by what is true. They have an evident tendency not to distinguish between the two."[1]

Many of us would both agree and disagree with Freud at this point. We know, by religious illusions he meant wish-projections, other-worldly orientation, supernaturalistic speculation. No doubt there will always be religious groups that find their strength and consolation in an other-worldly escape. In almost every congregation there are other-worldly escapists as well as this-worldly idealists who find it difficult to face and accept reality. Nevertheless, a large number of religious people are eager to know the truth and be able to distinguish it from falsehood.

Freud's claim that a group is subject to the magic of words[2] merits our serious attention. Our words may heal, but they may also injure. Our words may still the troubled waters, but they may also trouble the waters that need not be troubled. Inspirational atmosphere may be promoted by words that reach the depth of one's being, or it may be promoted by words of sentimentality.

It is tragic, yet true, that much of what has often been called dynamic preaching is only an exploitation of the surface areas of human emotions without ever reaching the depths of human life. When viewed from this perspective, Freud's *The Future of an Illusion* is not an angry battle against true faith and its manifestations; on the contrary, it is a fight against shallow, cheap, fanatic, illusory religious beliefs. Says Freud, "Man cannot remain a child forever; he must venture at least into the hostile world. This may be called 'education to reality.' Need I tell you that it is the sole aim of my book to draw attention to the necessity for this advance?"[3]

We can learn a lesson of great importance also from various experiments in group therapy. At times when preaching appears to be an administration of eye medicine to a patient on a street floor by a doctor on the twenty-fifth floor, it is good to remember the accomplishments of group therapy. To paraphrase the words of S. R. Slavson, it has changed many lives from egocentricity to other-love, from isolationism to participation, from neurotic anxieties to courage-to-be.[4]

For many months, I was trying to help a parishioner overwhelmed by problems of alcohol and divorce. When progress was not in sight, I suggested that she try group therapy at the state hospital in Islip, New York. The suggestion was accepted. Only two months later, Christine came home a changed person. She told me with rejoicing, "I would not want to drink now even if my bathtub were full of whiskey. After all, I am not a child anymore; I don't need to escape. I am thirty-five years of age. I should act and behave accordingly."

As Edgar Jackson has indicated, all these experiments in the field of group work have a direct bearing on the work of the pastor as preacher. "They verify the value of group method both in bringing inspiration and understanding. If the lecture method can help restore mental health to a group of seriously disturbed individuals, a carefully directed sermon can certainly do much more to help persons meet the milder disturbances of life with strength and understanding."[5]

## Making Way for Dialogue

As a young preacher, I was little concerned with dialogue in preaching. I knew people could not "talk back" to me and so "why worry about dialogue? Just proclaim the truth, and let it do its work." As the years went on, I came to see how erroneous my assumptions were. Today I know, we reach our congregation only by heart-to-heart, mind-to-mind, soul-to-soul search, communication, and dialogue. To paraphrase the words of R. E. Howe, dialogue is to preaching what blood is to the body. Without a dialogue our preaching is truly dead.[6]

In order that there may be dialogue in our services of worship, both the congregation and the preacher have to be on the same wave length. The preacher has to be ready for his congregation. The congregation needs to be prepared for a dialogue with the preacher. To accomplish this, we need to be constantly at work to remove whatever barriers to dialogue there may be. For our benefit, Reuel Howe has suggested six areas in which troubles might be located: (1) theological language; (2) images of one another; (3) anxieties—either personal or pertaining to the subject matter; (4) personal defenses; (5) contrary purposes; and (6) self-concern for being.[7]

One does not have to make an extensive study of religious concepts in our culture to discover that without clear and careful exposition many of them are "dead," empty, and meaningless to a large number of our people. Through teaching and pastoral calling, a minister discovers that even such frequently used concepts as heaven, hell, resurrection, redemption, God, Christ, grace, and eternal life are often empty of any concrete, empirical, personal meaning. Thus, if our listeners are to understand our language, these concepts need to be explained, interpreted, and filled with living meaning.

To go into depth, Earl H. Ferguson has pointed out that the use of abstractions is a serious roadblock to any communication. Says he, "The use of abstract terms in preaching, unless they are specified in terms of the particulars concerned by them, is not communication, but 'metacommunication.' It is the language we use when we do not know precisely what it is we are talking about."[8]

It cannot be said too often that a preacher needs to address himself to his people. The truth of the gospel is for the preacher as much as it is for all other worshipers in the congregation. When a preacher separates himself from his people by continuous references to "you" rather than "we," he has thereby lost a large number of his listeners.

A couple of years ago a college president came to our church and delivered a thoughtful sermon. He spoke on education and Christian faith. The sermon was scholarly in the best sense of the word. It was presented with clarity and conviction. Yet, the president made the sad mistake of setting himself apart from the rest of the worshiping congregation. Again and again he emphasized "It is your responsibility! You must do this and not forget to do the other." Never did I hear him say "We are called to this our mission. This is our task. We must do it together."

## Advance Planning

In his book *Fire in Thy Mouth*, Donald G. Miller has shown us how ridiculous it is to wait upon a last-minute inspiration.[9] Even if it came, it would not be an acceptable substitute for reading, study, research, planning, and preparation. The Holy Spirit was not promised to us to do our work, but to lead us into all truth. We owe it to our congregation and ourselves to prepare in advance. In our particular parish, we formulate a yearly program of preaching well in advance of the time when the first sermon of the series is to be delivered. Sermon topics, texts, subtexts, and scripture lessons are printed in a pamphlet which is distributed among the members of our congregation. First, the sermons are listed according to the series; then, according to the dates they are to be preached. Following is our current program of preaching:

PROPHETIC PREACHING

| | |
|---|---|
| "A Pioneer of Righteousness" | (Amos 5:24) |
| "Domestic Tragedy and Long-Suffering Love" | (Hosea 11:4a) |
| "Responding to the Challenge of God's Holiness" | (Isaiah 6:3) |
| "Incidentals or Fundamentals in Religion" | (Micah 6:8) |
| "Encounter with the New Covenant" | (Jeremiah 31:31) |
| "New Ideas about God" | (Isaiah 42:10) |
| "A Deep-Sea Adventure" | (Jonah 4:26) |
| "Beyond Reason and Compromise" | (Daniel 3:18) |
| "In the Valley of Dry Bones" | (Ezekiel 37:4, 14a) |
| "Escape from God's Retribution" | (Joel 2:13a) |
| "Answer from the Tower of Faith" | (Habakkuk 2:4) |
| "The Unmercenary Love of God" | (Malachi 3:10) |

## ADVENT

| | |
|---|---|
| "Advent Hope in Israel" | (Isaiah 35:2c) |
| "Messiah, Long Expected" | (Isaiah 11:2a) |
| "Fulfillment of Advent Hope" | (Isaiah 11:9a) |
| "Your Christmas Gift" | (John 3:16) |

## THE MAN OF NAZARETH

| | |
|---|---|
| "The Mystery of Incarnation" | (John 1:14a) |
| "The Son of a Carpenter" | (Luke 2:52) |
| "A Man of Prayer" | (Matthew 7:7) |
| "A Teacher from God" | (Mark 1:22) |
| "A Wholehearted Welcome" | (Luke 18:16b) |
| "The Extravagance of Love" | (Mark 2:17b) |
| "Acquainted with Grief" | (Isaiah 53:3) |
| "Crucified, Yet Risen!" | (Matthew 28:6a) |
| "God's Kingdom—A Paradox" | (Matthew 6:10) |

## THE CONCEPT OF GOD

| | |
|---|---|
| "God, the Power of Infinite Creativity" | (Psalm 147:5a) |
| "God, the Structure of Being" | (Acts 17:28) |
| "God, the Source of Wholeness" | (Romans 8:28) |
| "God, the Ultimate Destiny" | (Isaiah 52:10b) |
| "God, the Infinite Mystery" | (Romans 11:33) |

## RELIGION AND THE ARTS

| | |
|---|---|
| "Religious Problems in Contemporary Drama" | (Luke 19:40) |
| "Struggles of the Soul in Modern Novels" | (Ephesians 17b, 18) |
| "Affirmation of Faith in Contemporary Poetry" | (Psalm 139:7) |
| "Through Beauty to Holiness" | (I Chronicles 16:29c) |
| "Religion and the Sense of Humor" | (Ecclesiastes 3:4) |

## COMMUNION MEDITATIONS

| | |
|---|---|
| "United, Not Separated Brothers" | (John 17:20, 21a) |
| "The Symbolism of Eucharist" | (I Corinthians 11:26) |
| "Consecrated in Truth" | (John 17:19) |
| "He Accepted the Cup" | (Matthew 26:39b) |
| "Worthy Participants at the Holy Communion | (I Corinthians 11:28, 31) |

## AFTER ALL-CHURCH RETREAT

| | |
|---|---|
| "Sinners Called to Be Saints" | (I Peter 2:9) |

## REFORMATION SUNDAY

| | |
|---|---|
| "Thus a Religion Grows" | (Romans 12:2a) |

THANKSGIVING SUNDAY

"Criteria of Gratitude"                    (Psalm 100:4)

CHRISTMAS SUNDAY

"Your Christmas Gift"                      (John 3:16)

NEW YEAR'S DAY

"The Ancient of Days"                      (Psalm 90:2)

THE DAY OF PENTECOST

"Holy Spirit: The Fire of God"            (Matthew 3:11)

INDEPENDENCE DAY

"American Democracy and the Challenge of Atheism"              (Psalm 14:1)

This kind of preparation provides guidelines for sufficient study and research well in advance. It takes away our "text and topic anxiety." It enables us to find more appropriate illustrations. It gives the minister of music adequate time to prepare suitable service music. It helps the minister of education to select books for the leaders of youth forums who meet regularly after the service to discuss the morning sermon. It enables us to promote an integrated worship where all hymns, anthems, thoughts and prayers are united around the scripture text. It gives our congregation an opportunity to prepare for a dialogue with the preacher and one another.

## Recognizable Sermon Structure

Experience has taught that every sermon, however short, needs a clear, simple, and recognizable outline. Such outlines enable our listeners to follow our thinking and helps them to remember the thoughts and the ideas of our sermons that otherwise would be lost. Gene E. Bartlett has put it very effectively: "We have never been released from the basic requirements of unity, coherence, and emphasis in the establishment of structure for the sermon. When that structure is not there, a preacher can hardly hope to reach his listeners . . . Proclamation alone is not enough. The gospel needs a preacher simply because someone must put it in a form which can be communicated . . . The recovery of the gospel is important but so is its communication."[10]

Following are examples of outline structures I have used in many of my sermons:

1. Case, cause, consequence, cure in Christ.
2. Estrangement, sources, reconciliation.
3. Problem—alternative choices—solution.
4. Meaning, purpose, application today.
5. Parallel meanings.
6. What, when, why, and how.
7. Past, present, future.

## Effective Beginning

As I see it, our issue is not what comes first—the mind or the emotions. Both are inseparably related. Both belong together. What is truly important is our awareness that a dialogue must be established with the opening words of our preaching. When we fail to do this, our sermon may never reach a point of heart-to-heart communication. Harry Emerson Fosdick was a master craftsman in this respect. In his *Riverside Sermons* almost every sermon begins with an implied invitation: This is our problem. It can be solved. Now, let us reason together. Here are a few illustrations taken from *Riverside Sermons*:

> These are days when our lives go down into depths . . . Our thought this morning concerns our most serious moods. . . .

> We are concerned today about factual personal problems . . .

> Our subject probably takes us all in . . .

> One of the most important movements of our time is the gradual shift of emphasis from curative to preventive medicine.

> These are days when we need all of the resources we can find which assist in creating and maintaining mental health.

> There are three ways in which men get what they want—thinking, working, praying.[11]

## Dynamic Content

Most of us would do well to remember that it is not enough to establish a rapport with our congregation at the beginning and at the end of our sermons. It needs to be sustained all through our preaching. This we can do by various means and methods: a story, an illustration, an example, an acceptable humorous remark, or a noticeable change of posture or position.

Last year, a seminary professor came to preach at our church. His sermon topic might well be entitled "Faith and Protocol." It was an expository sermon on the book of Nehemiah. The topic alone did not sound very promising, yet the sermon was as dynamic and effective as it was profound in thought and dramatic and passionate in its presentation. The preacher started with a thought-provoking sentence. He moved quickly from one situation to another. He used his mind, his voice, his body, and his emotions to create and sustain our interest and attention. After he had preached for thirty minutes, he said his "Amen." The congregation looked up to him as if to say, "Oh no, you cannot do this. You must go on for we want to learn a great deal more."

As a native European, I find it difficult to employ much humor in my sermons. It is my understanding that a great deal of humor used in our sermons cheapens our gospel and may even distort our message. Yet, I am also aware that carefully chosen and properly incorporated humor may enable us to administer otherwise unbearably stinging medicine.

About a year ago, a missionary sponsored by our church visited us and preached to our congregation at both Sunday morning services. I will never forget the way in which he challenged us on our Christian world mission. He told us that while he was a parish minister in a city church he was as secular as many other preachers and congregations. He confessed that he did not then know the needs of these far-away people. He described how busy he had been organizing the various activities of his church. When he finished painting his picture of a preacher in a city church, one could easily sense a feeling among the worshipers: "What a shame! Our missions outlook has been so shallow and so unrealistic." I am sure, no one was resentful or hurt because the preacher "gave us a hard time." Most of his critical remarks were accompanied by a genuine smile—even laughter—and others were beautifully framed by his very delightful sense of humor. Clearly, with a smile, a touch of humor, and a glowing concern, almost anything can be said from the pulpit without ever distressing or alienating our congregation.

A dynamic sermon is one which contains at last one or two moving illustrations. It may be a description of a person, an event, a life situation, or it may portray a great struggle, a failure, or an achievement. The purpose of an illustration is always the same: to enlighten, to make clear, and to reach one's feeling as well as one's reason.

Here is a simple illustration used in a sermon aimed at helping some of the homeless refugees. This illustration is entitled "Am I Too Many?"

Some time ago, a displaced person sent me this letter. "The other day, we were discussing emigration. I told my wife that so many countries think they have enough of their own people. They do not want to have too many. At this instance my little girl lifted up her tiny voice with a most awkward question, emphasizing the 'I': 'Am I too many?'

"I know, we should not have talked before the children. But we have only one room. It is not that it is too little for us; when we sit all of us cuddled together on the old couch, it seems that we take no place at all, that the room is empty. Even with the several dolls included, no one here is 'too many.'

"And ten years ago, when this little girl was born as a daughter of a secretary of legation, there were roses sent by a senator, and his excellency, the American ambassador, patted the shoulder of a proud father and lifted his glass for a second time, saying something very cheery and very nice. No, she was not 'too many.'

"There is now in America a former lieutenant—a Quaker—who took candid interest in the destiny of us and our two children. Together with his parents, he arranged to find a sponsor for us. And there is the man who gave the affidavit of support—a manufacturer of shirts, also a Quaker, who has never seen us. When I show to my neighbor displaced persons the affidavit of support and tell them where it comes from, they exclaim one like the other, 'Is it possible that such people are still found in the world?' And they have tears in their eyes. And so had I; both my cheeks were wet when the affidavit arrived."

## A Sense of Authority with Compassion

The preacher who has done his pastoral work is sure to know that there is an unlimited number of human problems, both in the area of the Christian social gospel and in the field of the gospel called personal. There are theological problems awaiting examination, and there are political issues which need to be exposed in the light of our Christian faith. The choice of topics is always ours. It involves a profound responsibility. It should be attended with the greatest seriousness and thoughtfulness. It is up to us to discover a subject matter of greatest interest, urgency, and need.

Preaching with authority is preaching with a profound conviction and confidence. This is an important truth. It is substantiated by reason, revelation, and everyday experience. It needs to be said today. Our people need to know it. It will change their lives. It will answer their needs. It will make a positive contribution to our society. I have done my work of thorough preparation. God has given me this opportunity to present it. In his power and with his approval, I can do it.

Dynamic preaching demands an unusual measure of love, care, compassion, combined with a sense of urgency, authority, confidence, and conviction. Jesus possessed these qualities and so they said, "He spoke with authority and not like the scribes and the Pharisees."

## Deep-Level Preparation

Even the best prepared sermon can be a total failure unless as preachers we are personally spiritually prepared. Neither psychology, theology, philosophy, nor homiletics can ever substitute for our personal attunement with God. Our preaching is not made truly dynamic either by our knowledge of how to modulate our voice, how to shift our weight from one foot to another, how to raise our eyebrows or how to turn from laughter to tears. Dynamic preaching calls for personal honesty, sincerity, and commitment.

There is almost nothing more objectionable than artificiality in preaching. Speaking about another preacher, a parishioner once told me "he was totally intolerable." When I inquired "Why?" the answer was, "He did not mean what he said, and he did not say what he meant."

Stern is the judgment of James W. Clark, yet its medicine is much needed. Says he, "We flirt with our faith and philander with the solemn facts of interior experience."[12] Every Sunday we say directly or indirectly, "More things are wrought by prayer," only to discover later on that six days are not enough to set aside for private devotion and prayer. There are many devotional books of the quality of Kierkegaard's *The Purity of Heart,* Kahlil Gibran's *The Prophet,* and Russell L. Dicks's *My Faith Looks Up.* It is imperative that we set aside moments of devotional reading and self-examination.

Dynamic witness to God must be anchored in the supreme and ultimate dynamic of life. There must be oneness in our relationships with Him who hears and answers prayers. As we study and as we write, as we counsel and as we call, as we enter a home of a parishioner or step into the pulpit, we need to say with or without words, "Search me and know me, O God, and see if there be any wicked way in me, and lead me in the way everlasting. Take my thoughts and think thou in them! Take my words and speak thou through them! Take my hands and work thou with them! Take my soul and set it afire that it may proclaim thy goodness, thy power, and thy love!"

When we are angered by our own frustrations, when we are disappointed because we find that people are not what we expected they would be when we entered the Christian ministry, when we are inclined to think more highly of ourselves than we ought to think, when clouds of anxiety and despair appear at our own horizon, we need to come to God in repentance and surrender lest our preaching proceeds from unresolved conflicts, tensions, and turmoil and thus becomes destructive. Surrender is the secret of supreme dynamic in preaching.[13]

The power of God is manifest through the preacher only when he thinks more highly of God—his love, truth, wisdom, and power—than of himself. The preacher who has spent his busy week not only in reading and manuscript preparation, not only in business administration and church activities, not only in calling and counseling, but also in deep-level preparation with God, is destined to be ready to proclaim God's spiritual dynamic on Sunday morning.

**CHAPTER FOUR**

# PREACHING To The CRISES Of LIFE

The preacher who has done his calling and counseling knows that every Sunday there are parishioners in his congregation who are confronted with various personal problems and crises of life. They are eager to hear their pastor preach on (1) death and dying; (2) grief suffering; (3) physical sickness; (4) emotional illness; (5) loss of self-esteem; (6) marital distress; (7) handicapped living; and (8) problems of retirement age.

It is at such times that we are called to help our people become aware that God is a very present help in trouble. As the ground, power, and structure of life, he is immediately present. He is more real than the everlasting hills. His spiritual resources are unlimited. Through his power we can overcome every crisis of life. Following are outlines and excerpts on sermons dealing with various crises of life.

## Interpreting Death to Ourselves

*The Text:* "Even though I walk through the valley of the shadow of death, I fear no evil; for thou art with me; thy rod and thy staff, they comfort me" (Psalm 23:4).

*Introduction:* Death is a personal matter.[1]

Problems surrounding death must be solved by every individual for himself. Nevertheless, there are areas we can walk together in our reasoning about human finitude and death.

**Death is not our enemy.** It is high time that we emancipate ourselves from the idea that death is the punishment for sins. Human beings have always been finite. Whether death be brought about by terminal illness, old age, criminal passion, war, or an accident, it is not an absolute evil. Just think of the tragedy which would engulf us if we had to live on (forever) in spite of

44

incurable sickness, senility, or total paralysis. Death is not an enemy of life.

Death, certainly, terminates the activities of life which are dependent upon our physical body. After death there is no more seeing and hearing, no more walking and talking. As Jesus said, "After death they neither marry nor are given in marriage." By the same token, after death there is no more pain, no sorrow, no hardship, no troubles, no suffering. After death "these former things have passed away."

Death terminates many opportunities of living. Yet, if we are to rely upon reason and experience at all, if we are to be guided by personalities who have lived and finished their journey, we need not fear that death will undo what we have done; that it will destroy the values we have promoted; that it will turn our personal existence into nonbeing; that it will change our creative participation with God into ashes and dust; that it will destroy our identity.

Death is a great transformation; yet, it is a transformation only within the framework of God's laws, his power, and his love. Death has no power which is not delegated to it by God.

Clearly, the sting of death is in our separation from God, in our lack of faith and confidence in his goodness and love. The sting of death is in our spiritual decay, in our spiritual dying. As Paul has put it, "The sting of death is sin" (I Corinthians 15:56). It is guilt and sin and selfishness; it is anger, resentment, and bitterness; it is our inability to accept the limitations and the laws of life that fill our souls with terror and dread as we look at our own death and dying. We all have fears of death. Yet, they can be expressed and overcome.[2]

When we are sure of God's forgiveness, when we are aware of his continuous presence, we then can exclaim with great rejoicing, "Death is swallowed up; victory is won" (I Corinthians 15:54). We then can say with great confidence and conviction, "Yea, though I walk through the valley of the shadow of death, I will fear no evil, for thou art with me. Thy rod and thy staff they comfort me."

**Death—an adventure with God.** What is beyond our present life is a great mystery. It always will remain a great mystery, however much we would like to know its secrets. Apostle Paul has affirmed this in the following words: "Now we see in a mirror dimly, but then face to face" (I Corinthians 13:12a).

It is our Christian hope, however, that life after death will be a great realization, a great reward, a great reunion, and a great fulfillment. Some have tried to describe the details of this fulfillment and reward. Others have been and are contented to wait in hope.

Beyond death is a great mystery. What is certain to reason and faith at this point is that life must end in God for it has come from God. God is the Lord of life and also the Lord of death. Underneath are the everlasting arms of his love, wisdom, and power. God could never change himself to anything less than what he is now.

*Conclusion:* When we accept death in the framework of our Christian faith, we are ready to live.

After John Glenn had made his historic journey through space, he was asked questions similar to these: "What were your thoughts when you discovered that the heat shield of your space ship was in trouble and that possibly in your reentry you would melt in a 3,000-degree temperature? Were you terrified? Were you afraid? Were you praying? How did you feel?" The answer of our beloved astronaut was something like this: "I was not terrified. A long time ago, I had made peace with my Maker." Unafraid to die, he was fit to pilot our space ship, Friendship Seven. Only if unafraid to die are we really fit to live.

## Courage for Days When Health Fails

*The Text:* "Be strong and of good courage . . . for it is the Lord your God who goes with you; he will not fail you or forsake you" (Deuteronomy 31:6).

*Introduction:* God has not promised us perfect health. He has promised us courage and strength for days of illness.[3]

**Courage listens to reason.** About ten years ago, I knew a woman who was the heart of her church school. She was loved and respected by all of her pupils. She was equally much admired by members of her Christian community. Her reputation was beyond reproach. She was praised by all. Yet, her life was cut short by a disease that the doctors said could not be cured. Helen was a victim of cancer.

Among the finest ministers that I have had the privilege of knowing personally and intimately, there are many who have suffered from ill health. To me, it would be almost blasphemous to think that their suffering was punishment.

I never had the privilege of knowing personally the Reverend James A. Huff, a member of our community who was destined to live through unspeakable suffering and agony. Those of us who have read the life story written by his wife[4] are convinced he was a man of God. He firmly believed that sickness is neither the expression of God's anger, nor the work of the devil.

In sickness and in health, God is constantly with us. He is the Great Sufferer who understands. Those who suffer, and have suffered, belong to a great fellowship in which Christ has a place of honor. When sickness and ill health are understood in this way, our courage is bound to increase. It is strengthened when we begin to think as Paul did that "endurance produces character, and character produces hope, and hope does not disappoint" (Romans 5:3–5).

*Courage listens to faith.*    In a primitive form, healing is associated with shamanism. Some of the reflections of this shamanism are detectable even today in various adventures of the so-called "miraculous healing." Yet, faith healing does not have to rely upon superstition, magic, and shamanism.[5] The ministry of Jesus was to a large extent a ministry of healing.[6] The testimony of those who were healed by him is to be understood as we would understand our own testimony of healing given in faith, looking in retrospect. Yet, even with this admission, there is no doubt in my mind that Jesus brought health and healing to many who came to him in prayer and faith.

Some of our greatest physicians and professors of medicine have come to affirm their faith in the healing powers that are available through faith. Dr. Claude Forkner of Cornell University says, "We do not know what it is that brings about the recovery of a patient. I am sure, however, that often it is faith which is a most important factor."[7]

The Bible would be much poorer indeed if all the references to God as a source of health and healing were removed. Therefore, if courage for days of illness is what we need, let us turn faithfully to the words of the Scriptures and saturate our minds with them and live (Psalm 46:1; Psalm 27:14; Isaiah 40:10; Malachi 4:2; Psalm 23; Deuteronomy 31:6).

*Courage listens to love.* "Each act we perform from motives of love pours strength and health into the stream of life."[8] Through love our natural courage is elevated to the level of heroic strength. There is available to me from personal experience an episode about a very sick woman who came to a service of prayer for healing. Together with another very ill person, she went up to the altar to have her minister pray for her. When she arrived there, she totally forgot herself; and, seeing a person suffer emotionally, she began to pray: "Dear God, please help my suffering friend." God answered her prayer and gave her strength through love.

Our real tragedy in sickness is self-absorption. We forget that there are others who suffer—maybe more than we do—that there are others who need our help. We magnify our troubles. In our prayers we ask God to heal us. We forget to pray for the comfort, the healing, and the peace of mind and soul of others.

*Conclusion:* Act upon the promise of God.

Here is a story about a Negro minister who had to undergo surgery. Shortly before his operation, an orderly committed an almost unforgivable sin. He told the Negro preacher, before he was taken to the operating room, that his roommate had just passed away on the operating table. The nurses were panicky and alarmed. Yet, nothing could be done to change this situation. The patient was operated on, and, in a short time, he returned. At seven o'clock in the evening I called on him and said, "You probably were terribly alarmed when you heard that your roommate had passed away on the operating table." He said, "Yes, but only for a moment. Then, with my eyes closed I saw Marian Anderson with her arms outstretched singing 'He's got the whole wide world in His hands.' Thus, I went to sleep, and thus I awoke after the operation. The whole world is in His hands."

## Troubled by Emotional Disorders

*The Text:* "You will know the truth, and the truth will make you free" (John 8:32).

*Introduction:* Many of our emotional troubles are deep. They are anchored in our lack of self-knowledge, repressions of all sorts, failure to relate ourselves to persons, failure to communicate with and surrender to God. Behind all our strange, unexplainable fears, anxieties, guilt, and depression are deep-seated reasons.[9]

**Inheritance from early childhood.**   In his book entitled *Light Beyond Shadows*,[10] Dr. R. Frederick West tells us a heartbreaking story of what happened to him just because in his early days he had heard his father say, "We really did not want him; we wanted a girl." Apparently, his feelings of rejection, created by these carelessly spoken words, haunted him throughout his college days, throughout his teaching profession, and even into the ministry, until it finally exploded with very damaging results.

The authors of *Spiritual Therapy*, Richard K. Young and Albert L. Meiburg, relate for us a very enlightening confession. These are the words of an unhappy man who could not get along with others. Said he, "Preacher, you just can't depend upon people these days . . . I have had enough. I have even thought of speeding in my car and then jerking the wheel so that it would be all over . . ." As the preacher probed deeper in this man's soul, the man went on to say, "Yes, my father was the boss in our family. He told us how to do the job and we were expected to do it right. It was hard at times to keep from getting lickings because I wanted to haul off and tell him what I thought, but I never did."[11]

Apparently a deep-seated resentment against his father and a fear of him had frightfully incapacitated the man. He had repressed many a feeling into his unconscious being. His soul had been damaged.[12]

A few days ago I met a gentleman who could tell me a great deal about religion. Yet, when I spoke to him about the importance of church life, he said that he did not have any particular need to belong to a church. Said he, "I have had enough. When I was still very young, my father, who was a minister, made me read the Bible several hours a day—especially on Sunday afternoons." His negative attitude toward the church was set at the age of six.

A deep, long look into the mirror of our childhood experiences is sure to release us from some of the poisonous contamination of our feelings and lead us a long way toward God's liberating truth. We are restored to wholeness when we recognize our enemies within, whether they be an indiscriminate need to please others, overvaluation of a partner, belittling of ourselves, craving for power and prestige, dread of failure, or relentless driving for perfection.[13]

*The forces of our culture.* As Vance Packard has shown us in his book, *Hidden Persuaders,* we are living in a status system where the most motivating force in the lives of many is the so-called social mobility—the aspiration drive, the achievement drive, the drive to be successful.

We let ourselves be brainwashed by "hidden persuaders," by "architects of salesmanship." First, we listen, though we know that many an advertisement is totally untrue and absurd. Then, we begin to believe, and we listen on. "Stop taking whatever you now take. Switch to my product, for it has a miracle ingredient. It will work like magic . . . If you want to move up the social ladder, move up to my intoxicant. It will put you out of your misery. It is used by all status suckers everywhere . . . If you are young and a speed devil, you must buy my hot rod . . . If you have arrived and are established, you must buy a car of 'distinction' . . . If you do not want to work (and no one should work hard except the communists), you must buy the soap that does everything with less and less and less toil . . . And if you believe in purity, as all good housemothers should, you must stick with Purity Products . . . If you care for good luck, watch for the good luck image on all our merchandise . . . And if you want the smoke that satisfies, you must buy the tobacco that has been imitated yet never duplicated, for all the baseball pitchers smoke our brand and nothing else . . ."[14]

As a result, we press on to reach the top of the ladder. We command our inner voice to be silent. We repress our guilt, fears, and doubts. We put one mask upon another until our true self is totally buried. And when we sense an inner explosion coming, we reach for a tranquilizer when we should be looking for a minister, a counselor, a man who knows and understands the disorders of the emotional and spiritual life.

Even worse than emotional illness is our stone-age philosophy that emotional and spiritual disorders are the work of the devil, that they cannot be healed, that a man cannot be restored to full health and strength and wholeness. Even worse than emotional illness is our turning away from the person who needs an assurance that there is a "balm in Gilead." "You shall know the truth, and the truth shall make you free."

***Restored to spiritual wholeness.*** It is not my intention to dispute the idea that unless security, harmony and love were placed in our cradles, we are destined to wander in hopeless insecurity and despair. When we look at Christ, we know this need not be so.[15] His childhood was not an example of security. His early home was often threatened by hostile forces. He was more misunderstood than many others. Even his parents could not fully understand him. He often worried and puzzled them.

Yet, instead of having a timid and insecure feeling, he taught and spoke with authority. Instead of being aggressive, he was humble, patient and loving. His moral fortitude could not be defeated even on the Cross of Calvary. God's love and power had made him strong.

We are restored to spiritual wholeness when we realize we need God's help. We are made whole when we accept his love and his healing.

*Conclusion:* God can heal you now.

*Out of the Depths*[16] is a living testimony of God's healing power. To Dr. Anton T. Boisen the struggle for sanity was a prolonged one. Yet, he finally reached the promised land of freedom and creativity. The words of our text were fulfilled in his life. They have been fulfilled in the lives of many others. They can be fulfilled in your life and mine.

## *Alcohol—A Stumbling Block*

*The Text:* "Wine is a mocker, strong drink a brawler; and whoever is led astray by it is not wise" (Proverbs 20:1).

*Introduction:* There are three types of drinkers.

According to an article entitled "The Great God Bacchus,"[17] all drinkers may be classified in three categories. First, there is the casual drinker. Alcohol is a part of his life, but not an important one. He can take it or leave it. On the second level, we find the problem drinker. Alcohol plays a very important part in his life. He needs his bottle to enable him to face his problems: family, financial, social, occupational, and recreational. To him, alcohol is a crutch without which he cannot walk. The third category embraces the chronic alcoholic. For him, alcohol is more important than anything else. He is ready to sacrifice every value, however sacred, merely to continue the satisfaction of his urge for alcohol. He is a sick person.

***Alcohol is basically a depressant.***   It is evident that alcohol as an euphoriant has a very limited value. When taken in small amount, it may serve as a catalyst in social gatherings. It may liberate the timid from the rigid restraints of his superego. It may remove awkwardness and tension. Yet, basically it is a depressant rather than an euphoriant.

"Alcohol," says Dr. Robert de Ropp, "is a protoplasmic poison with a purely depressant effect upon the human nervous system. After it has passed from the blood into the brain, it acts first on that area of the cerebral cortex which exerts a restraining action on our more native impulses. To use Freudian terminology, it puts our superego to sleep. As a result, the tongue-tied may become eloquent, the shy may grow bold, the awkward may become graceful. At the same time, the mean may become vicious, the unpleasant may grow ugly, and the angry may become ferocious. Much, of course, depends upon the character or the type of the individual under consideration."[18]

***Alcohol is a mocker.***   When consumed in larger measures, the depressant influence of alcohol exerts itself on those areas of the brain which regulate movements. The drinker acts foolishly; yet he thinks he is smart. When the concentration of alcohol in the blood stream reaches .2 percent, the entire motor area of the brain is affected. "At this state," says Dr. de Ropp, "our boozer may be called 'beastly drunk,' although such an epithet is really an insult to the beasts. He is unable to stand upright; he is also prone to ridiculous display of emotions in which he alternates between senseless rage and senseless tears."

When the percentage of alcohol in the blood stream reaches .3 percent, "the drinker's brain is affected in that area which is concerned with sensory perception." He has little comprehension of what he sees, feels, and hears. When the percentage reaches .4 to .5 percent, the whole area of perception in the brain of the drinker comatose. If the percentage becomes .6 or .7, "our drinker dies a swift and painless death." For an effective illustration I refer you to the story about Mrs. S., related by Robert S. de Ropp.[19]

***A source of manifold troubles.***   The problem of alcohol does not end with the damage it exerts upon the alcoholic—his physical body, his nervous system, and his life in general. No alcoholic lives in a vacuum. There are families, friends, and fellow citizens who are bound to be trapped in the circle of tragedy.

According to statistics, alcoholic hangovers cost our industries more than $1 billion a year. It means 400,000,000 man-hours' loss of time. It amounts to $125 million in preventable accidents.

The total number of people that are directly affected by those who misuse alcohol is estimated to be over 20,000,000. How many of those are fathers and mothers, how many young children and teen-agers, how many husbands and wives, how many college students, we do not know. We only know, all of them are involved in a circle of tragedy beyond words and description.

*Conclusion:* Seek help and anchor your life in God.

With faith in God we can face our life situation. We need not lose our self-esteem. We can rebuild our inner strength to resist an invitation to escape.

## Marriage Can Be Reconstructed

*The Text:* "Unless the Lord builds the house, those who build it labor in vain" (Psalm 127:1).

*Introduction:* Marital distress.

The withering away of family life is one of the most tragic encounters in our otherwise rich, prosperous, and progressive civilization. Divorce cases have grown to unbelievable proportions. Infidelity is no longer considered a shocking experience. Large numbers of people have become frustrated and maladjusted. Immaturity has increased. Emotional unbalance is growing. Our social relations have become deeply disturbed.

***There are deep reasons.*** As Smiley Blanton has indicated, behind it all are deep reasons. "When marriage fails, the specific complaints invariably turn out to be merely pretexts. They are masked expressions of profound psychic hostilities whose inception goes back to the hates and resentments of early childhood."[20]

We are troubled because many persons have entered marriage with a reservation: "We will stay married if it works; if not, we

will divorce." They have started without knowledge, without preparation, without listening to reason.

We are troubled because our views of sex have often been
shallow, unhealthy, and unholy. There are fanatics on both sides.
And there are misunderstandings of all kinds.

A very tragic story about marriage without love and understanding is told by Dr. Blanton. Here is a business executive. His income, $75,000 a year. He is married, yet desperately unhappy. He
is unable to relate himself in intimate matters to his wife. He lives
by a concept that there are two kinds of women—the lower type
meant for sex, and the higher (his wife), for respect and adoration.
What an ignorant view of sex! And yet, how many people are
there in the category of similar ignorance.

**Religion is basic to reconstruction.**     All along, there is wisdom
and help in the teachings of Christ. Sex "freedom" is no freedom.
Divorce is bad, but sometimes even worse is mixing together
people who do not belong together. Exploitive relationship is personally and socially destructive. By wrecking one home, the adulterer
weakens all homes; he affects all families; he brings about a curse
on children and youth. All forms of loveless marriage come to the
same thing—a corruption of the heart, a destruction of the home, an
end of real happiness. Marriage must be built on love which embraces eros, filia, and agape—the greatest of these being love which
bears, believes, and hopes all things.

**Love must be cultivated.**     As a tender plant, love needs to be
cultivated daily—when working or at rest, when doing our shop-
ping or teaching our children, when entertaining guests or pre-
paring for a vacation, when making our plans for the future or discussing our past and our differences of opinion.[21]

Not long ago a middle-aged couple came to discuss their marital
problems. The woman was ready for separation. Her husband re-
sisted the thought. He said he loved his wife. Yet, when I asked him
to be specific, he gave no answer. I enumerated a dozen instances
where his love could have been expressed. Every time, his answer
was negative. Together we learned their marriage could be reestablished only if they were willing to cultivate love in practical
ways and thus open their lives to the love of God.

Conclusion: The family that knows something greater than itself, the family that knows God's resources and strength, the family that is united in the observance of God's law of love, the family that is guided by rational rather than emotional thinking is bound to stay together and experience happiness.

## Growing Old Gracefully

*The Text:* "But grow in the grace and knowledge of our Lord and Savior Jesus Christ" (II Peter 3:18).

*Introduction:* Here is a prayer for the middle-aged person given to me by a friend:

Lord, thou knowest better than I do that I am growing older and some day will be old. Keep me from getting loquacious, and particularly keep me from the fatal habit of thinking that I must say something on every subject and on every occasion.

Release me, O God, from craving to try to straighten out everybody's affairs. Make me thoughtful but not moody; helpful, but not bossy. With my vast store of knowledge and wisdom, it seems a pity not to use it all. But thou knowest, O Lord, that I want some friends at the end. Keep my mind, O God, from the recital of endless details and give me wings to get to the point.

Seal my lips on my own aches and pains. They are increasing, O Lord, and my love for rehearsing them is becoming sweeter and sweeter as the years go by. I dare not ask, O God, for grace enough to enjoy the tales of others' pains, but help me to endure them with patience.

Teach me the glorious lesson that occasionally I may be mistaken. Keep me reasonably sweet. I do not want to be a saint, O God, for some of them are so hard to live with, but a sour old person is one of the crowning works of the devil. Keep me where I can extract all possible fun out of life. There are so many wonderful and funny things, and I do not want to miss any one of them. Amen.

Think with me for a moment about the phrase, "Keep Me Reasonably Sweet."

Life's supreme tragedy is not poor health, lack of wealth or beauty or great gifts, a disappointing marriage, or having a boresome job to do, grievously hard as these may be to bear. It lies in the fading of our youthful vision, and our greatest sorrow is ever the death of that sparkling, water-clear spirit of wonder we possess as children, that keen joy in the world and in all living, that pure faith and believing heart, that bubbling of the divine joy within us.[22]

Whatever our age, we dare not let our laughter go. Our sense of humor has much to do with our physical and emotional health. It is healthy laughter that often enables us to overcome moodiness, self-pity, and self-conceit. It is laughter that often washes our eyes from unnecessary tears and helps us to see things with a better vision and from a higher perspective. It frees us from anxious cares and destructive tensions.

Vitamins are good, of course, and pep pills may sometimes be necessary. Yet, under given circumstances, no better medicine can be found than laughter and a sense of humor. Even Christ practiced that.[23]

By humor we tear down the walls of isolation and establish friendships. There is no time in our lives when we can afford to overlook the spiritual significance and the cultivation of our sense of humor. Especially, we need to be aware of this as we advance in age and maturity; for as long as we can smile and use our God-given humor, we can be sure no one will regard us as the crowning work of the devil. We will not be rejected. We will be wanted, loved, and accepted.

*Wings to get to the point.*    I know a friend who has a special need for much talking. I wanted to visit him as his pastor. Yet, I was afraid that I would never get out of his house. Like an automaton he would go on and on, reciting endless details of his past experience. I am sure he had never thought about the prayer, "Keep my mind, O God, from the recital of endless details and give me wings to get to the point."

There are other people besides us who have their problems and their troubles. We need not always be able to lift their burdens from their shoulders or solve their riddles. We need not always be able to transform their lives as we wish they were transformed. Yet, we can listen with forgiving and understanding minds. We can pray that God will enable them to solve their problems. Instead of ignoring, repudiating, criticizing, or condemning them, we can show our increasing concern and love with words of hope and encouragement.

If we are to grow old gracefully, we need to learn day by day to think less and less of our own troubles and more and more of the needs of others who still have a long way to travel. We need to pray God for listening ears, understanding hearts, pleasant words "sweetness to the soul and health to the body."

*The secret of acceptance.*  All of us are called to work for the coming of God's Kingdom. Yet, we have not been asked to straighten out the affairs of every person. God did not impose his wisdom on us in an authoritarian fashion. He gave us opportunities to learn and to discover things in our own way. He treated us as sovereign individuals. He trusted us. This attitude we need to cultivate toward others—whether they be children, young people, middle-aged persons, or older men and women.

In order to grow old gracefully we need to learn "how to die and keep on living." We need to keep our hearts and souls free from resentment and bitterness, especially as we are called to witness the collapse of some of our brightest hopes. We need to learn to refrain from blaming God and others, especially when called upon to go through the defeats, disappointments, setbacks, suffering, and the tragedies of life. According to an old established maxim, men are not killed by the adversities of life. They are destroyed by their inability to accept them and to transform their evil into good.

*Conclusion:* God's grace is available at every age. Curiosity, joy, outgoing concern need not die at the age of ninety. In our own congregation we have a living example of this truth. One of our members reached his ninetieth birthday. Every Sunday he is at our services of worship. To all of us, he has been a source of inspiration and a reminder that God's grace is always sufficient. God's grace is available at every age!

## Thank God for Your Troubles

*The Text:* "In everything give thanks: for this is the will of God in Christ Jesus concerning you" (I Thess. 5:18 K.J.V.).

*Introduction:* We are grateful for self-evident blessings. We rejoice over good health, happy family relations, high social status, rewarding work, material prosperity. We do not give thanks for troubles, handicaps, and limitations. This we should not do.

*Limitations are extraordinary lessons.*  In German, a gift is "gabe" while a lesson is "aufgabe." Troubles are God's aufgabe—the gift of a lesson.

Behind my extraordinary hardships (and there have been many: escape from behind the Iron Curtain, experience in Hitler's labor camp, struggle for survival in a burning city, adjustment problems in a strange culture), I heard God say: "Now, here are some hardships; see what you can do with them—a lesson for your life."

We had just come to this country and were surrounded by new culture, new language, new traditions, new customs, new life. All of it made our start rather difficult. The first book assigned to my reading at the seminary was *The Romance of the Ministry.* Not a very difficult book to read, yet it was difficult then. As I struggled through it with the aid of six or seven dictionaries, a friend of mine from the seminary walked in and said, "What are you trying to do? You will never finish the assignment! The book has a couple of hundred pages. You can read only three pages an hour. And you have only two days to finish the assignment. Why don't you give up!" I told my friend that language inadequacy was an irresistible power that moved me on.

When God wants to educate us, he sends us to the school of hardships and limitations, for no other school can accomplish the task.

Schiller produced his greatest tragedies in the midst of physical pain. Handel composed his greatest music under the stress of suffering and death. Mozart composed his *Requiem* while fighting a fatal disease. Beethoven created his greatest music when oppressed by almost total deafness. Victor E. Frankl became convinced of logotherapy in a death camp.

Fanny Crosby was blind; yet, we are told that she produced more than three thousand hymns, among which are the familiar ones, "Pass Me Not, O Gentle Savior," "Rescue the Perishing," "Savior More than Life to Me," and "Jesus, Keep Me Near the Cross."

It is a fact of life that even in prison cells great literary works have been born, such as *Robinson Crusoe; Pilgrim's Progress; The Life and Times; No Cross, No Crown; The History of the World;* some of the epistles of Paul; and lately, a great epistle written by Martin Luther King, Jr.

*Obstacles are unusual opportunities.*  When God wants to

make a person great, he confronts him with obstacles of life. Well has it been said by Orison Swett Marden: "Adversity exasperates fools, dejects cowards, draws out the faculties of the wise and the industrious, puts the modest to the necessity of trying their skill, awes the opulent, and makes the idle industrious."[24]

*Farewell to Fear* is an incredible story about a blind girl who now skis, climbs mountains, and plays golf. We are told that she manages a thriving business enterprise and is one of the most popular lecturers in America.[25]

In his autobiography, *The Living of These Days,*[26] Harry Emerson Fosdick tells us about a very disturbed man who came to him for counseling. The visitor told him that he was going through the most dreadful hell anyone could portray. He began to describe his feelings of fear and frightening depression that surrounded him. The counselor interrupted him saying, "Don't you tell me how you feel. Rather, listen to my description." And so he went on. The patient listened for a long time. Then he said, "And how do you know it all so well?" He knew it so well because he had experienced it and was able to help in a special way. There had been a hidden blessing in his tragedy.

***Limitations are blessings in disguise.*** Just the other day, I picked up a magazine entitled *Faith at Work*. I opened it, and my eye was caught by an article on "My World Collapsed." Here was a story about a man who had started life with cerebral palsy. Against this terrible background he had built himself an amazing stamina, determination, and courage. Says he, "I could be as intellectual as any—witty, alert, crafty, jolly, and whatever the occasion demanded. Then one night something dreadful happened. My self-made world collapsed. I felt as if my mind were being pulled away from me." He tells us that his fear was indescribable. He was overwhelmed with a sense of absolute meaninglessness, and terrifying darkness. In his agony, he turned to God for the first time in his life. God answered. Through failure and tragedy, he discovered resources of priceless value for life. He learned to surrender to God.

Yehudi Menuhin is a famous violinist. He tells us that during the second World War, he was invited to play for some forty wounded soldiers in a hospital in the Aleutians. When he arrived there, and his accompanist sat down at the piano, they discovered that half of the keys on the instrument would not play. He was in a predicament. Without the piano he could not play the scheduled compositions of light music. Immediately he thought about the music of Johann Sebastian Bach. Yet, he knew that Bach would be difficult to comprehend. He hesitated for a moment, and then he played. When the music was over, he received a tremendous ovation. The soldiers had not only been entertained; their hearts had been stirred, moved, and inspired.

*Conclusion:* Handicapped and grateful, you belong to spiritual nobility.

Ours is not a perfect world. Many times we suffer hardships and limitations for which we have no explanation. There is mystery which hangs over our existence, too deep for us to penetrate. Yet, the truth remains: The valley of tears, poverty, failure, misfortune, and handicap is also God's workshop where human greatness is created.

### Under the Strain of Grief

*The Text:* "Blessed are those who mourn, for they shall be comforted" (Matthew 5:4).

*Introduction:* All of us are subject to grief. In our grief, we are not alone. The whole world is with us. There are husbands and wives, fathers and mothers, brothers and sisters who have suffered before. In times of bereavement we need to remember it is *natural to vent our emotions.*

Lazarus had passed away. He had been a personal friend of Jesus; so, we read, "and Jesus wept." The women who came to the grave where Jesus was laid were weeping when they found their Master was not there.

When I learned that my father had suddenly died behind the Iron Curtain, I closed my study door and let my emotions speak.

A pretense that our feelings are unhurt by a sudden death of a friend or a loved one is foolish and dangerous. We do not need to pretend. Rather we need to express our sorrows, to manifest our grief, to speak our mind, to share our thoughts with others. See a minister! See a friend! Unburden your soul!

**It is healthy to express our grief.** In times of bereavement we are all destined to wonder "Why, why did God permit this to happen now?" A fine woman, aged sixty-nine, came to me and said, "Why did not God permit my dad to live just one more year? He was doing so well." I knew her father was ninety-one years of age at the time he died. Yet, I did not say to her, "Oh no, he was already quite old." Instead, I said to her, "Naturally, you loved your father so much. It is not easy for anyone to take a loss like this. Yet, we must be ready to face the full reality. Courage comes to us as we refuse to look for detours around the truth."

In times of bereavement all of us are bound to encounter some feelings of guilt. Our opportunities to do anything for our loved one are over. Looking in retrospect, we are sure to find instances where we could have done much better. We need to find forgiveness. At the same time we need to be kind to ourselves. "Withdraw the emotional capital from the past."[27] Only as we withdrew can we face the future.

In times of bereavement, we are in a state of emotional crisis. As long as it doesn't last for weeks and months, it is a normal human experience. We need not be alarmed.

In his book entitled *Peace of Mind*, Joshua L. Liebman has made this suggestion: "Do not be ashamed of your emotions. Do not be afraid of breaking down under the strain of your loss. The pain that you feel now will be the tool and the instrument of your later healing."[28]

***Hold on to your faith in bereavement.*** God is with us always. He hears our prayers and is more willing to give us strength to overcome than we are to pray. We only need to pray in an affirmative way and remember his promise: "They who wait for the Lord shall renew their strength, they shall mount up with wings like eagles, they shall run and not be weary, they shall walk and not faint."

All of us are familiar with the tragic yet magnificent story about Peter Marshall. His death, we are told, was a profound shock to young Mrs. Marshall. It came at the height of his career. Yet, as we learn from the book *To Live Again*,[29] through love, faith, and trust in God she conquered her grief and found her way to meaningful living. And so can we.

***Our equilibrium will be restored.*** There are many things we can do to enable God to help us. We can look at our loss from an outgoing point of view. We can concentrate our efforts to help other grief sufferers. We can seek new activities, new interests, new relationships. We can assure ourselves that we will be comforted by God. Our emptiness will be filled with meaning. New relationships will be established. We will have new opportunities of creative freedom. Life will be worth living. Hope will open the door.

*Conclusion:* Remember the words of Tennyson's *Ulysses:*

> Though much is taken, much abides. And though we are not the strength which in olden days moved earth and heaven, that which we are we are . . . One equal temper of heroic hearts, made weak by time and fate, but strong in will to strive, to seek, to find, and not to yield.

## CHAPTER FIVE

# MINISTERING To The SPIRITUALLY ISOLATED

Frank Laubach has said it with conviction: "It does not matter how big heaven is; it matters how big our pipe is and whether it is open. The bottleneck is never God; it is always ourselves."[1]

There are many parishioners in our Sunday services of worship who have isolated themselves from the power and the love of God. Their spiritual channels have become blocked. As preachers, we are called by God to help them "break the log jam." In our preaching we need to be concerned with those who are (1) overanxious; (2) guilty; (3) lonely; (4) discouraged; (5) hostile; and (6) bored.

Following are outlines and excerpts from sermons dealing with the problems of spiritual isolation.

## Living Through Anxiety

*The Text:* "In the world you have tribulation; but be of good cheer, I have overcome the world" (John 16:33).

*Introduction:* All anxieties are not alike. Some are rational; others, temperamental. Some anxieties are morbid; others, existential. Each has a different source.[2] In order to overcome, we need to recognize their origin.

***Anxieties anchored in faithlessness.*** We worry about our children, health, reputation, job, income, age, looks, appearance, and a multitude of other things because we lack faith that God is, that he cares, that he will supply our needs in time of crisis.

A medical doctor, whom I have respected and admired, said he had to live in an old, broken-down, rented home because he did not have enough money to buy a new house. When I said, "You do not need the whole amount but only a down payment," he protested saying, "I could never buy a house on mortgage. Anything could happen to me. How would my family take care of it?"

If all of us regarded life from such a perspective, our living could not continue. Surely, there will be troubles. Yet, God will be with us. We need to learn to live one day at a time and leave tomorrow to his loving care.[3] Most of the troubles we expect never happen. Many, when they do happen, are not as bad as we anticipated. We often worry in vain.

We are created for happiness and fullness of life. Both include responsibility and care for others. Yet, God does not want us to carry the world on our shoulders. He does not want us to feel responsible for the choices and decisions of others.

The vicious cycle of anxiety, hostility, and guilt is broken by our entrance into the reality of brave, adventurous relationship with God.

***Anxieties anchored in guilt.***   Some time ago, a very unhappy couple came to talk to me about their intimate relations. Both were dreadfully anxious, upset, and fearful. They were convinced that they had done something wrong. For many a year, they had suppressed their feelings. When the pressure was too strong, they came for help. Evidently their guilt was overwhelming. They wondered if God would forgive them. They needed someone to listen and say, "Though your sins are red as scarlet, they shall be white as snow."

Failures, mistakes, and troubles of life are inescapable. Worse than these is our perfectionism—inability to forgive God, forgive others, and forgive ourselves. There is deep truth expressed in this caricature of prayer: "Dear God, I have forgiven you your big blunders; now, please, forgive me my little waywardness."

God is not stricken by our limitations. He is the source of wholeness. He understands. He accepts us though we may think ourselves unacceptable. He is ready to forgive us.

***Anxieties anchored in self-centeredness.***   In his *Channels of Spiritual Power*,[4] Frank Laubach tells us that out of 186 persons who were interviewed at a summer camp in New Hampshire, 78 complained that they felt they had blocked God's spiritual power by their self-centeredness.

It is our ego worship that keeps us in the prison of anxiety. What we need is to let ourselves go in the realization that we are not the earth and the sky, nor are we the center of the universe.

When God's love is blocked within, it becomes spiritual indigestion, a source of anxiety. When we begin to care for others, we are destined to experience healing in our own hearts. Love is the answer to many an anxiety.

*Conclusion:* Give to the winds your fears! Write your worries in the sand!

What tomorrow will bring we do not know. Whether our path will be smooth or there will be signs: "No Exit" or "Dead End," we do not know. We can be sure of one thing only: God will never fail!

In his book, *Achieving Real Happiness*,[5] Kenneth Hildebrand tells the story of a woman who was afraid of burglars. One night, when a burglar did come and her husband had given him the requested money, he then said to the burglar, "Mr. Burglar, my wife is upstairs in dreadful agony of fear. I will call her downstairs to meet you; she has been expecting you for the past twenty years. She will be surprised to learn that you are not as terrible as she thought you would be." This is an experience all of us can tell with many variations. What we need, therefore, is to give to the winds our fears, to rest and be assured. Sufficient unto the day is the evil thereof.

## Surrounded by Loneliness

*The Text:* ". . . Yet, I am not alone, for the Father is with me" (John 16:32).

*Introduction:* Loneliness—characteristic of our age.[6]

In each of us is a thirst for dialogue, communication, togetherness, fellowship, and meaningful participation in life. Yet, so often our spiritual hunger and thirst remain unsatisfied. We do not know how to say what we know we ought to say. We do not know how to relate ourselves to God and others. Our efforts of togetherness are blocked. We become uprooted. We are blown by the winds and storms of life. We float on the surface. We cry, "My God, my God, why hast Thou forsaken me?"

***Major source of loneliness is within us.*** We are lonely because we think and believe we are not wanted, not loved, not appreciated, not accepted. We do not admit to ourselves that the source of our feelings of loneliness is to be found within. Rather, we project this into the outer world. For our loneliness we blame either our loved ones, our neighbors, or even the church. We think they are cold, unfriendly, selfish, and hostile. In reality, it is only a projection.

Some time ago a woman came to me and said, "Pastor, you don't know what it means to be lonely. I am at the end of my road. No one will talk to me. No one will say to me 'Good Morning.' No one wants to be with me. They still believe that I belong to the communist underground of which I was once a member. It was all a mistake. Yet, they have not forgiven me." Probably they had not forgiven; yet, it was clear to me that neither had this dear woman forgiven herself for the mistakes she had made. The guilt and the insecurity of her own soul had cut all lines of communication with others. She was totally and desperately lonely.

We build our walls of isolation by various means: by fear and suspicion, by resentment and insecurity.

We suffer from loneliness because of negative evaluation of ourselves. Instead of working to full capacity, we behave as though we were inferior, stupid, and unappealing. Says Dr. Earl Loomis, "A child who fears he won't be liked never finds out how likeable he would be. A young girl who believes she is so unattractive she'll never have a date actually contributes, by worry, to the poor appearance that fulfills her fear. The student who is excessively fearful about passing examinations inhibits his study to such an extent that he does fail. A woman who fears she cannot love God ultimately flees from even the thought of Him."[7]

All of this leads to destructive isolation. Ours is a decade of great progress. Yet, we often suffer from dreadful loneliness because our "foundations have been shaken." We begin to think that the universe is essentially unfriendly and antagonistic to the quest for life's meaning. We begin to doubt that there is any rationality, any purpose, any sustaining order, any law that governs this universe. We begin to concentrate on human finitude and the insignificance of our existence. As a result, we are overwhelmed by a sense of loneliness and despair.

**Loneliness can be overcome.**  For the loneliest soul, there is salvation. And here, self-understanding is basic. We are true to others when we are true to ourselves. Our existence is affirmed as we affirm the existence of others. When we accept others as they are, we achieve a confirming relationship that is acknowledged by the familiar address, "thou." It is in this "I-thou" relationship, as Martin Buber has explained, that loneliness begins to vanish.[8] For an excellent illustration I refer you to the story told by Mary Tully.[9]

"A little boy went to lunch with his mother and sister in a restaurant. After the sister and the mother had given their orders, the waitress turned to the boy and asked, 'Young man, what will you have?' But before he could reply his sister said, 'I'll order for him.' The waitress repeated her question to the boy. But again his reply was stifled, this time by his mother, who said, 'I'll order for him.'

"The waitress, undaunted, repeated her question to the boy. 'Young man,' she said firmly, 'what will you have?'

" 'A hamburger,' the boy said.

" 'And how would you like it? Rare, medium, or well done?'

" 'Well done.'

" 'And what would you like on it—mustard, pickles, onions, relish, or catsup?'

" 'Mustard, pickles, onions, relish, catsup—the whole works!'

"The waitress repeated the order, 'One hamburger, well done, coming up—with mustard, pickles, relish, onions, catsup—the whole works!' And then she walked off to fill the orders.

"The boy turned and exclaimed in astonishment to his mother, 'Gee, Mommy, she thinks I'm real!' "

We may overcome our loneliness by talking it out with someone who understands. A very intelligent young man came to me the other day and told about his personal problems. After he had told me the whole story, I said to him, "I know exactly how you feel, for I have felt the same way myself." Not much more was said at this visit. Yet, when he left the office he said to me, "You have lifted my burden a great deal." When he was gone, I asked of myself, "What burden did I lift from his shoulders?" And in my own mind, I could see no other burden more real than the burden of loneliness.

We can overcome our loneliness by lifting our innermost troubles to God in prayer, for with God is strength, healing, help, and encouragement. As Dean Miller of Harvard has put it, "Prayer is a thousand things, but it is always the meeting of God and man, and at that moment there is peace that passeth understanding." In such a communication we are destined to be relieved from our anxiety and resentment, from fear, guilt, suspicion, and sin. We are bound to know the deeper meaning of the words of Jesus, "Yet, I am not alone, for the Father is with me."

*Beyond loneliness.* Jesus was often alone but, being alone, he was not lonely. In the struggle of Gethsemane, he was alone. Being in agony, he prayed most earnestly. His sweat was like great drops of blood falling to the ground. Yet, he was not forsaken. "There appeared an angel unto him from heaven, strengthening him."

Even on the cross he was not absolutely overcome by loneliness. He was lonely for a while as he cried, "My God, my God, why hast thou forsaken me?" Yet, shortly thereafter his heart was filled with an assurance of God's presence and acceptance.

*Conclusion:* Triumphant in solitude.

Even in solitude we would triumph over our loneliness, as many a saint, martyr, and mystic has done before, if with every atom of our being we would believe that "in Him we live and move and have our being"; that "underneath are the everlasting arms"; that "He is above us, beyond us, beneath us, around us, and within us to give us strength"; that "He will never leave us nor forsake us."

## Make Sure You Are Forgiven

*The Text:* "For if you forgive men their trespasses, your heavenly Father also will forgive you; but if you do not forgive men their trespasses, neither will your Father forgive your trespasses" (Matt. 6:14, 15).

*Introduction:* God's forgiveness is unlimited.

Forgiveness of God is such that it is forever available to all of us regardless of how many mistakes we have made, how badly we have failed, how rebellious we have been, how far we have gone. God was ready to forgive the prodigal son, the adulterous woman, the tax collector, the outcast, the criminal sentenced to die on the cross, even the proud and self-righteous Pharisee (Isaiah 1:18; 44:22).

When the prodigal son returned to his father, no questions were asked. In love he was welcomed and received. God's forgiveness is of the same quality. No questions are asked. Yet, it is such that it may be limited by us.

*We must recognize the need to be forgiven.* How many people there are in this world who actually believe that they are perfect, sinless, self-sufficient, always right, we do not know. But we do know there are people who regard themselves as self-sufficient. We call them self-righteous Pharisees. We feel sorry for them. They are excluding God's forgiveness and, thus, are unable to forgive.

True forgiveness begins by recognizing the evil and by confessing our natural reaction of anger. When both the evil action and the feeling of anger are borne before God, forgiveness and recovery of our inner peace become possible.[10]

Christian forgiveness is not the same thing as a stoic-like leniency, endurance, and serenity, that we can develop by constant self-discipline and self-training. Christian forgiveness comes as a gift from God.

To obtain it, none of us can pray too often, "Lord, help me to know if there be any pride or vanity within me." For pride is one of the subtlest, cleverest and the most damaging of our inner orientations. So quietly and unnoticeably it takes over the driver's seat and makes forgiveness impossible.

We cannot ever pray too often, "Teach me, O God, to know the areas of my soul that are unsurrendered to Thee, the areas of my being where resentment and rebellion are building their weapons of destruction." We cannot pray too earnestly, "Help me, O God, to know and understand my anger, envy and bitterness."

*God's forgiveness depends on our forgiving others.* This may not be self-evident. Yet, Christ has taught us that God cannot fill with love and forgiveness an unforgiving soul. Our anger and bitterness on one side and God's love and mercy on the other are mutually exclusive.

It is almost useless to ask God's forgiveness if there be any unforgiveness within us toward others. Jesus said, "Leave your gift there before the altar and go; first be reconciled to your brother, and then come and offer your gift" (Matt. 5:24).

Such is God's forgiveness that it comes from God to our brothers, and from our brothers to us, and then it is made real in us when we forgive. Since there is a wall of separation between us and our neighbors, God cannot make his forgiveness meaningful within us.

***Forgiveness depends upon our readiness to accept it.*** We do not need to persuade God with either long or short prayers. For the Psalmist says, "He knows our frame" (Psalm 103:14). He is more ready to give us good things than we are to pray. All we need is to persuade ourselves to open our innermost self to God's love and mercy. The forgiveness of God is as free as the sunshine from above and as available as the air we breathe.

We need not cry aloud, day and night, that God would manifest his forgiveness as though he were hard of hearing or far way from us. "In him we live and move and have our being" (Acts 17:28). The Psalmist affirms it: "Thou dost beset me behind and before, and layest thy hand upon me" (Psalm 139:5).

Such is God's forgiveness that we need only to build a spirit of affirmation and acceptance within ourselves to experience it. It is this affirmation we find over and over again in our Scriptures (I Chron. 29:11; Isaiah 6:3; 54:10).

*Conclusion:* Move on to forgiveness.

Try to understand! It is not as bad as you think it is. Accept yourself! Forgive yourself! Accept others in the same way! Don't experiment; forgive! Forgiveness is miraculous! When did you say it last: "You are forgiven?" Do it now, and you will be forgiven.

## Let Hatred and Malice Go

*The Text:* "You have heard that it was said, 'You shall love your neighbor and hate your enemy.' But I say to you, Love your enemies and pray for those who persecute you" (Matt. 5:43, 44).

*Introduction:* Various reactions.

In numerous ways people have responded to these words of Jesus. Those who agree with some of the teachings of Confucius would say, "If we are to reward evil with good, curses with blessings, hate with love, with what are we to reward love, goodness, and kindness?"

Many more have reasoned, and probably we ourselves among them, that this kind of teaching presupposes human perfection. And since none of us could truthfully claim to be capable of it, the words could not be taken with too great a seriousness. Besides, we know our feelings are ambivalent. The sooner we recognize it, the better. Hate is only the opposite pole of evil. Both are bound to remain with us as long as we live.

The practical man in us is convinced that this kind of idealism does not work. He is convinced that this is not the way to abolish crime, corruption, injustice, and various forms of social evils. And so he tells us that this probably will be practicable and applicable only in the ideal society. Yet, the aim of Jesus remains unshaken. In our religion we must transcend hatred. We must transcend the orientation according to which even God is conceived in terms of wrath, anger, and hate. In Numbers we read: "The anger of the Lord was kindled against the people, and the Lord smote the people with a very great plague" (Num. 11:33).

In Psalm 106, verse 40, it says that the wrath of God was so kindled that he abhorred the people whom he had created because they were so utterly wicked.

In Deuteronomy, chapter 29, verse 28, we find that "the Lord uprooted them from their land in anger and fury and great wrath, and cast them unto another land."

Since these people believed in the wrath and indignation of God, it was quite rational for them to justify their own anger, hate, and bitterness. Thus, in the 139th Psalm, we find a reference where a man speaks about "a perfect hatred" and "perfect malice," obviously directed against the nonbeliever.

To Jesus, this justification was nothing short of blasphemy. He knew no holy hatred, no sacred malice, no divine anger. Against the religion of anger and malice he directed his new commandment of love. If he came to us today, again he would say, "It was said to you, 'hatred may be religiously justified.' I tell you this is patent falsehood." The religion of hate is destructive. It cannot solve any problems, or reduce any tensions, or reconcile fighting men and nations. It cannot fill human hearts with joy and peace.

To pray for those who despitefully use us, to bless those who curse us, to do good to those who hate us is utterly impossible unless God is believed to be the God of love. We can forgive only if we ourselves have felt the need of forgiveness and have experienced it in our own hearts.

If Jesus came to us, he would say again, "Whatever you think, or pray, or say, or do, don't ever justify hatred and malice in the name of God!"

*Our justice must be without vengeance and retribution.* The law of retaliation was regarded as a guiding principle in all human relations in the olden days of Hammurabi. Its code of ethics prescribed that a giver should receive as much as he gives. The same was said in different words in the old Jewish law: "an eye for an eye, a tooth for a tooth." In essence, this is punitive justice. Jesus proposed something better than that. He taught us to overcome hatred with love.

Jesus was not opposed to the courts of justice. Without them life would be unlivable. He did not denounce the use of police force, for mankind was not then nor is it now on a level high enough to do so. Jesus did not suggest that we abolish our defenses. He did not say, "Bless every wicked thought, movement or philosophy." He was concerned with personal human relations, with a higher type of justice than a punitive one. Hatred cannot promote pardon. Vengeance cannot create kindness. Malice is unable to improve human relations. Jesus suggested that we take off the draperies of self-righteousness. For it is self-righteousness that blocks our understanding, forgiveness, and love.

Psychological studies have revealed that it is hard for us to conquer malice, vengeance, and hate because behind them are repressed resentments, frustrations, and pride. People who feel that life has denied them their due are bound to remain prisoners of vengeance and hate. And even so, our repressed resentments are bound to break out into hate. No less damaging are our own frustrations. However, there is an answer. Hate is overcome by creative love.[11]

W. L. Northridge tells us a story about a boy whose parents had a strange habit of visiting their family grave on Christmas. The little boy disliked it intensely because it meant his giving up playing with toys. Yet, he too had to go. His father was an old "dictator." There was a deep resentment in the boy's heart. When the family returned from the cemetery, the boy built a snowman in the image of his father and pelted it with snowballs in great anger and hate.[12]

Because of our imperfections, our subconscious forces, and our imperfect society, we may never be able to measure up fully to the commandments of Christ our Lord: "Bless those who curse you;

do good to those who hate you. Pray for those who persecute you." Yet, it ought to be clear to all that unless we are willing to seek redemptive rather than retaliatory justice, we do not belong to our Master's company.

Our conquest over hatred, malice, and vengeance begins with *an outgoing prayer, whispered in love.*

When we are powerful enough, we may be able to silence, defeat, or even destroy our enemies; but we can never change and transform them, or make them our friends, except by love, kindness, and blessing.

In self-defense, we may repeat the words of the fisherman: "It ain't given to human nature to be so kind, good, and loving." Yet, the truth is that unless we hope, dream, and pray for the fulfillment of that new commandment of Jesus, neither we nor the world can ever come closer to the kingdom of righteousness and peace.

As Paul Tournier has said, hatred and love are related as $-N$ is related to $+N$. Hatred can be replaced and overcome only by love. Life is like a tennis game. It never finishes if you always return the ball. If you can forgive, the balls can come your way without your having to send them back.

*Conclusion:* Look at the Cross and pray!

A woman who was badly hurt by a character assassin came to her minister and said, "I do not know what to do. My soul is deeply injured. I wish I could, but I cannot forgive." In deep concern the pastor said, "Why not fix your eyes on the Cross of Christ. Be silent and let his cross speak to you. Then offer a prayer to God and say: 'Dear God, You do know everything. You know what "X" has done to me, and how much it hurts. Help me to understand her need to seek gratification in such vicious gossip. Her husband is such a dreadful disappointment to her. Her life is so miserable. Show me what I can do to return goodness for her evil. Make me a channel of thy love.'" God answered that prayer the very moment it was said.

## Discouraged by Grim Powers of Darkness

*The Text:* "Why dost thou make me see wrongs and look upon trouble? Destruction and violence are before me; strife and contention arise" (Hab. 1:3).

*Introduction:* Believers are troubled.

Evil is a profound issue only to those who believe that God is, that he loves, that he cares for us, that he is omnipotent, and that his goodness is at the heart of this our universe. Such believers, together with Habakkuk, are often driven to ask: "Why dost thou show me evil?"

We are troubled by natural disasters of all kinds. We are disturbed by wastefulness involved in the evolutionary process and by purposeless surds of all kinds. We are hurt by ills that fall upon human life like hungry vultures. We are heavy laden by tumors, cancers, and arthritic pains, by heart troubles and emotional disorders of all kinds. We are often startled by human corruption and degradation, by ruthlessness, brutalities, injustices, and the apparent triumph of wrong over right. The words of the poet, James Russell Lowell, seem to echo over and over again in our hearts: "Truth forever on the scaffold, wrong forever on the throne." Yes, why dost thou show us evil?

***Our problems are beyond absolute solution.***   The problem of evil is so complex that only in pride could we expect an absolute answer. Around it there is a great deal of mystery which we are not able to solve. It is rightly stated in the Scriptures: "Now we see in a mirror dimly, but then (when with God) face to face." Paul Tillich has put it this way: "No description of the structure of evil can be exhaustive. It is an infinite task."[13]

According to H. E. Fosdick, the chief reason why his father wanted to go to heaven was "that he might get God off in a corner and ask some questions." The problem of evil is a gigantic one. Yet, the magnitude of it would be greatly reduced if we would only remember that behind many so-called intrinsic surds are positive rather than negative principles. It would greatly help us if we would see, in the first place, that *sensitivity determines both—pleasure and pain.*

In his omnipotence, God could have freed us from our sensitivity. He could have created us without our feeling nature. If he had done this, we would not be hurt by any thing mean or ugly. Never would we mourn in sympathy, disappointment or identification. Nothing would ever provoke or excite us. Yet, if God had taken away our sensitivity and our feeling nature, neither would we be able to enjoy anything, for pleasure rests upon the same foundation as pain. To great music we would listen, yet without any inspiration. To the beauty in nature our eyes would be opened; yet, it would never thrill us. Sports and recreation would have no attraction for us. There would be no rejoicing in anything. No tears—no laughter! No pain—no pleasure! Our life would then be reduced even below the level of speechless creatures. This, however, God has not done!

He has given us the capacity for gladness and rejoicing, love and sympathy, laughter, pleasure, and happiness. To ask for these without the possibility of suffering would be equal to asking for sunshine without shade, felicity which we do not deserve. We suffer pain because behind both—pleasure and pain—is God's wonderful gift of sensitivity and feeling.

In the second place, the magnitude of the problem of evil would be greatly reduced if we would remember that *human freedom is behind both—good and evil.*

In his omnipotence, God could have created us ready-made angels, without the possibility of making any mistakes. If he had done this, the world would know no crime, no corruption, no dereliction of duty. Sinfulness, rebellion, and disobedience to God would be nonexistent. No one would ever make a wrong choice. All conflicts, struggles, and strifes that tear out human hearts would be eliminated. War would be impossible. No man would ever suffer injustice and humiliation.

At the same time, also abolished would be our freedom to choose between right and wrong, truth and falsehood, good and evil. We would then be elevated to the level of mechanical angels.

If freedom were taken from us, we would lose our personal dignity and worth. There would be no real learning, no growth, no progress, no overcoming, no necessity for divine grace and salvation, no newness of life, no spiritual triumph and victory. This, however, God has not willed. He has given us freedom. He has bestowed upon us the possibility of knowing the difference between right and wrong, truth and falsehood, good and evil. And with this, he has qualified us for his grace and salvation. Yet, the price for these precious gifts is the possibility of a wrong choice.

Finally, the magnitude of the problem of evil would be greatly reduced if we would remember that *our antagonists are also our helpers.*

No doubt God in his omnipotence could have abolished all of our antagonists—all forms of physical and mental troubles, all secular atheistic and demonic forces, all hardships and obstacles. Yet that would mean the reduction of life to nothingness. For as W. MacNeile Dixon has put it in his book, *The Human Situation*, "It is through the contraries and in no other way, that our thought is encouraged, intelligence heightened, consciousness intensified."[14] These antagonists are "the hounds of heaven" hunting us, that we may develop all of our powers. This has been gloriously demonstrated by noble souls throughout the ages.

In 1810 a young lad came to his mother and said, "Mother, may I have a hundred dollars?" The mother answered, "Son, we have a piece of land, eight acres in all. It is rough, hard, and rocky. It has not been cultivated. Now, in twenty-seven days you will be sixteen years of age. If by that time the field is plowed, cultivated and planted, you will have earned that money." In this very hard beginning was the secret, I believe, to the colossal fortune made by Cornelius Vanderbilt.

Our antagonists are also our helpers, for they that wrestle with us, strengthen our nerves and sharpen our skills. It is through suffering that we learn sympathy, love, and understanding. It is through hardships that we grow in courage, strength, and determination.

It may seem that truth is always on the scaffold, wrong is always on the throne; yet, the poet knows more than appearance. He knows reality. For "that scaffold sways the future, and behind the dim unknown, standeth God within the shadow, keeping watch above his own."

No antagonist in its own power, and by necessity, is capable of separating us from the ground and the power of being (Rom. 8). Not even in existential estrangement, caused by our selfish pride, concupiscence, anxiety, guilt, doubt, and despair—not even in the state of condemnation—are we ever totally separated from the power of God which works in us for good in all things.

"Yes," says the author of *Faust*, "to this I hold with firm persistence; the last result of wisdom stamps it true: He only earns his freedom and existence who daily conquers them anew."

*Conclusion:* Let us summarize and take courage!

Ours is an unfinished world. As a result, many things may appear to be basically evil in it. Yet, this is not so. For through its incompleteness, we are given a chance to grow and to be co-workers with God in creative adventures.

Ours is a world of opposites. Thus, we may think that it is basically dualistic, that half of the world is good and half of it evil. In reality, it is monastic and united. For behind every set of opposites is God with his goodness. Evil has no independent existence. It is only the shadow side of good.

Ours is a world of freedom. Often, however, our choices are wrong. Consequently, we suffer from our partial estrangement from God and cry in despair, "Why dost thou show me evil?" Yet, even through this agony of soul, God's grace is made sufficient to us. For if only we were willing to listen, these words of assurance we would hear with clear perception: "Behold, all things work together for good for those who love God."

## CHAPTER SIX

# CONCERNED With LIVING MEANING

The preacher who has been in communication not only with his parishioners but also with "the world" knows that Christian faith is gravely challenged, doubted, and disputed by many people. The most common religious terms—such as God, Christ, heaven, hell, redemption, resurrection, and eternal life—have become meaningless clichés, shibboleths, and husks of a previous culture to many of our contemporaries. Others are faithfully holding on to the old Christian concepts but are uncertain about their meaning. A large percentage of our people are anxious to hear us preach on (1) Christian Communication; (2) God's Word and the Bible; (3) The Reality of God; (4) The Meaning of Prayer; (5) Miracles Old and New; (6) Hell and the Day of Judgment; and (7) Resurrection and Eternal Life.

Following are excerpts and outlines of sermons dealing primarily with meaning.

## Christian Communication[1]

*The Text:* "To you it has been given to know the secrets of the kingdom of heaven" (Matthew 13:11).

"Blessed are your eyes, for they see, and your ears, for they hear" (Matthew 13:16).

*Introduction:* Religious language is symbolic.[2]

The language of faith is destined to be symbolic because religious life is inseparably bound together with its roots in the past, its hopes for the future, its search for the depth of meaning. To portray the depth, vitality, and richness of divine-human encounter, Jesus always spoke in parables. Take any one of his parables as an example.

Religious language is bound to use analogy, myth, and metaphor because a great deal of our living is anchored in the subconscious, subsensuous, sublinguistic levels of life.

The language of faith is destined to remain symbolic because by means of religious symbols we open the doors to the Eternal. It is this orientation that made Paul Tillich say, "When God as symbol was lost, God himself was lost."[3]

Our question remains: "How are we to understand religious symbols, parables, analogies, and myths? How are we to attain the status of those to whom Jesus said, 'To you it has been given to know the secrets of the kingdom of heaven. Blessed are your eyes, for they see, and your ears, for they hear.' "

In the first place, we must put ourselves in *the position of the narrator*.

At this point, the knowledge of history is of paramount importance.[4] Apart from our knowledge of the history, for example, of Israel and Judah, the book of Jonah may appear to be a simple tale. A prophet swallowed by a whale—nothing but a "fish story!" Yet, when we become acquainted with the history of the Hebrew people, the book of Jonah becomes an allegoric epic of great significance.

The prophet: the Hebrew community; the fish: the Babylonian monster; the three-day exile: three exiles of the nation—one in 722 B.C., one in 597 B.C., and one in 586 B.C.; the return of Jonah: the return of Israel; and then the gigantic struggle for a belief in a God who is full of mercy (Jonah 4:2).

Only against the historical background can we fully understand the language of faith, for example, of Habakkuk, II Isaiah and Ezekiel. As we listen to their words, let us remember, the two were exilic prophets (Ezekiel 37:1-5).

Our undestanding of the New Testament demands the same. The Gospel of John, for example, is bound to remain an unsolved mystery, with its language about the Logos that was in the beginning, unless we know the time and the place where it was written and the Alexandrian philosophy which it presupposes.

We must also remember that while the proclamation of "The Word" involves acts and events of history, while religious language is, in a way, determined by events of history, the kerygma itself goes always beyond the portrayal of history. It is a portrayal of *an inner experience with God*.

The language about the beginning of the creation is certainly not a description of an historical event as we understand history. No one was there to witness God's creative activities at the beginning of time. No one was there to hear him call for the sun and the moon and the stars. No one was there to witness the creation of the earth and the sky and the seas and the mountains. The creation story is a testimony of one's faith in God the Creator.

The Biblical proclamation of the birth of Jesus was not primarily a description of an historical event. It is a proclamation of faith describing an inner experience so well put in these words: "For God so loved the world that he gave his only Son, that whoever believes in him should not perish but have eternal life" (John 3:16).

The kerygma pertaining to the resurrection of Jesus is not a proclamation of what happened to the human body of the Master. Deeper, much deeper, it is a description of the resurrection experienced in the soul. Christ himself being present and speaking, "Peace I leave with you; my peace I give to you; not as the world gives do I give to you. Let not your hearts be troubled, neither let them be afraid" (John 14:27).

The Book of Revelation is not a blueprint of the size and the shape of heaven. It is a book that speaks about one's depth experience with God. It speaks about the meaning, the purpose, the joy, the hope, and the courage that can be found in "fellowship with the Father."

An understanding of religious language requires an awareness that symbolic and approximate is every description of *objects of ultimate meaning and significance.*

Numerous are the symbols used in the Bible to describe the source of every blessing, the ground and the power of being, the end of our pilgrimage. In the Book of Psalms he (God) is often spoken of as the Lord (Psalm 8), as a strong tower, a rock of salvation, a refuge in times of troubles, a king, and a judge to reign forever and ever.

No word in our human language can adequately describe the infinite, the transcendent-immanent, the omnipotent, the all-wise, the all-loving, and the all-merciful God. He is beyond the reach of our highest thought; yet, paradoxically enough, he is also with the heart of the lowliest.

The same is true concerning the Kingdom of God. It is an experience that goes beyond words. It is a new relationship—a relationship where the first is the last and the last is the first, where the least is the greatest and the greatest is the servant of all!

*Conclusion:* Blessed are those who see, hear, and understand! Theirs is the Kingdom of God. For illustration I suggest the poem by Walter Rauschenbusch, "The Little Gate to God."[5]

## The Bible and the Word of God

*The Text:* "Thy word is a lamp to my feet and a light to my path" (Psalm 119:105).

*Introduction:* The Bible, a book of spiritual wealth.

There are many chapters, statements, and references in the Bible that may be of great interest to a student of history, archaeology, physics, biology, astronomy, as well as to a student of psychology, philosophy, sociology, or literature. On all of these subjects, separate books similar to the one enititled *Bible As History* could be written.[6]

Yet, the Bible is not to be read primarily as either a great masterpiece of literature or a textbook of science or history or philosophy. To do so is to misunderstand it and misread it.

"It is both ridiculous and disgraceful," says Emile Brunner, "when the theological apologetic, which for 200 years fought against Copernicus, Galileo, Kepler, and Newton, in the name of the Bible, now that the matter has been decided against it, maintains that there is no conflict at all. There is no doubt that there is a conflict . . . The modern science of astrophysics proves that the geocentric view of the Bible is untenable."[7]

"Man's knowledge and mastery of the world have advanced to such an extent that it is no longer possible for anyone seriously to hold the old Biblical view of the world; in fact, there is hardly anyone who does it."[8]

The Bible is a book of spiritual wealth. Yet everything in it is not of the same spiritual value nor or on the same level. "The moral standards and the religious insights of the barbaric tribes who swept through Palestine before making it their own were different from those of their descendants after the prophets had shown them more of the nature of God and his purposes for man."[9]

The Bible is an inspired book. Yet, it is not, and cannot be taken to be, literally and verbally inspired. For God is not the source of inconsistencies, errors, contradictions, lack of knowledge, and lack of love. He is perfect in wisdom, in power, in love, and purity.

**The Bible, man's search for God.** As no other book in the world, the Bible gathers and expresses the ageless and timeless groping and longings of the human soul for someone beyond itself—for God. It is here, on the pages of the Scriptures, that we become acquainted with men who in their long, long hours of sorrow, suffering, loss, failure, hardship, and struggle, in the depth of their souls sought for an explanation of why these things should be.

Here, on the pages of the Bible, we meet with people who are praying, hoping, and waiting for their liberation from guilt and sin and shame (Psalm 51). Here they are struggling to understand the will of God and the meaning and purpose of life (Isaiah 40:6-8). Truly, a lamp unto our feet and a light unto our path.

**The Bible, an unfolding of God's own revelation.** God has not always spoken the same way to all generations. This an omniscient God could not and would not do. In the book of Hebrews we read, "In many and various ways God spoke of old to our fathers by the prophets; but in these last days he has spoken to us by a Son" (Hebrews 1:1, 2a).

On these pages of the Bible, we find an unfolding revelation of God himself. At first we see him believed to be limited geographically and spiritually. He was conceived to be a god of storm and war and one in human fashion. He was regarded as a special guardian of his people of Israel. Then, thanks to the prophets, he becomes the God of righteousness, mercy, and loving-kindness.

Still, God continued revealing himself until it became clear to the men of the Bible that "God is spirit, and those who worship him must worship in spirit and truth" (John 4:24). "God is love, and he who abides in love abides in God, and God abides in him" (I John 4:16b). "No one has ever seen God" (John 1:18); "In him we live and move and have our being" (Acts 17:28); He is indeed the reward of all our seeking.

The Bible is an unfolding revelation of moral ideas. We begin with tribal justice and primitive morality: an eye for an eye, a tooth for a tooth. We move on to the ethics of the New Testament.

"Let all bitterness and wrath and anger and clamor and slander be put away from you, with all malice, and be kind to one another, tenderhearted, forgiving one another, as God in Christ forgave you" (Ephesians 4:31,32). From morality formalized in legalism and ritualism and priestcraft, we move on to individual ethics. We advance from external to inward morality (John 3:3). (Romans 12:2). The ordinances of the law are "fulfilled in us, who walk not according to the flesh but according to the Spirit" (Romans 8:4). "If anyone is in Christ, he is a new creation" (II Corinthians 5:17).

Here we see an unfolding revelation of human suffering. We begin with an idea that happiness and health and success are due to the favor of God, while misery, poverty, failures, and troubles are the much-deserved punishments for sin. And many years it took until God could disclose to his people that suffering is an essential part of human life and divine nature itself; that sacrificially borne, suffering is redemptive.

The aim of life is not to abolish suffering, for that would abolish sensitivity. The aim is merely to abolish cruel, barbarous and useless forms of suffering, to elevate and sublimate its expressions, to make it creative and redemptive.

Here is also an unfolding revelation on eternal life. Clearly, the Hebrews believed in life hereafter. Yet, to them it was to be a shadowy existence—a very different outlook from what we find in the Gospel according to John: "He who believes in me, though he die, yet shall he live" (John 11:25).

**The Bible, a portrayal of divine drama.**   In their struggle for freedom, the people of Israel were not alone. God was with them. He said to Moses, "Depart, go up hence, you and the people whom you have brought up out of the land of Egypt. My presence will go with you . . ." And Moses said to him, "If thy presence will not go with me, do not carry us up from here" (Exodus 33:15).

In their fight for justice, loving-kindness, mercy, and holiness the prophets were not alone. God was with them in their struggle. And God said to Jeremiah, "Do not say, 'I am only a youth'; for to all to whom I send you you shall go, and whatever I command you you shall speak. Be not afraid of them, for I am with you to deliver you."

In their exile in Babylon, the Jewish people were not alone. God was with them. In their battles, he fought with them, he suffered with them, he triumphed with them. Said he: "When you pass through the waters I will be with you; and through the rivers, they shall not overwhelm you; when you walk through fire you shall not be burned, and the flames shall not consume you" (Isaiah 43:2). See also (Isaiah 40:10,11).

*Conclusion:* The Bible, a Testimony to the Word of God.

God's word is God's power unto salvation. The written record is not the same as the living reality. Yet, indisputably, for centuries even the written record has been a channel of grace.

It happened in 1944. Compelled by powers beyond our control, my wife, my three-year-old child, and I had to leave our native land—the land of our fathers for hundreds of generations—our church, our home, and everything that we called our possessions. The one thing we would not leave behind was the Bible in our native tongue, given to us at the Service of Ordination. All through the days of our exile it was "a lamp unto our feet and a light unto our path." Amen.

## God, Our Contemporary

*The Text:* "Whither shall I go from thy Spirit? Or whither shall I flee from thy presence? If I ascend to heaven, thou art there! If I make my bed in Sheol, thou art there!" (Psalm 139:7, 8).

*Introduction:* True God is inescapable.

There are a great many idols and god substitutes before whom a multitude of people bow down in fear, trembling, and humble submission. There are numerous ideas which many regard to be of ultimate importance and significance, even though they cannot give meaning, purpose, and power to our being. There are many things in human experience, such as pleasure, status, and peace of mind, which have often been put on the throne on which the Almighty God alone is entitled to be.

According to the Psalmist, to worship them is plain idolatry. The only God who is worthy of our ultimate concern is the God from whom there is no escape. The only God who is worthy of our adoration, praise, and respect is the God who can threaten or bless our existence and being. And it is this God that the Psalmist describes in our text: "Whither shall I go from thy Spirit? Or whither shall

I flee from thy presence? If I ascend to heaven, thou art there! If I make my bed in Sheol, thou art there!"

**God, our Creator.**   The Semitic people who lived three thousand years ago were speaking about God the Creator in very anthropomorphic terms. They conceived him in human fashion. He had eyes to see and ears to hear. He had hands to work and feet to walk. For them and for himself, he planted a garden and walked therein in the cool of the day. He had the same feelings they had. He was pleased and angered. He was jealous and impatient. He was wise, and when he had made mistakes, he was repentant. When all his creative work was done, he was tired and needed rest.

Today, our understanding of God is different. We speak of him as the source of cosmic power which continuously calls forth new worlds into being, which continuously creates new galaxies, new milky ways, new stars, new forms of life. Nature, we know, is not a static collection of atoms. It is a creative process. The creative work of God continues. He is equally the God of the microcosm as he is the God of the macrocosm. He is the God of the telescope as well as the God of the microscope. And there is no place where we can hide from him.

Today we speak of God as cosmic intelligence, the source of all the wisdom behind the rational structure of the universe. An atheistic scientist may deny his existence in words; yet, he is forced to affirm it in action, for without that structure there cannot be science or research; there cannot be discoveries; there can be only chaos, darkness, and nothingness.

God is the giver and the keeper of all the laws of the universe. The time may come when chemists are able to produce life in a test tube. Yet, the time will never come when they will be able to create new laws or even one iota of the laws of the universe. The giver and the keeper of the laws is God. Without such laws, the world would have come to an end a long time ago.

Trillions of living cells are a testimony to the rationality of the universe, the creative powers of God, the reality of an all-inclusive, creative intelligence from which there is no escape.

**God, our Redeemer.**   Obviously, God is not a person as you and I, unless we want to return to the level of anthropomorphic thinking about the eternal God. God is not like one blade of grass among others, one star among others, one tree in the forest, one grain of sand on the ocean shores. He is the Creator of all the forests, the flowers, the stars, and the milky ways. He is greater than any person you or I can possibly imagine. He is the source of individuality and personality. From Him there is no escape.

To have faith in God is to believe in the power of spiritual and personal transformation. All things can be made new. Our lower nature can be changed. With God we can overcome our selfishness, immaturity, pride, and greed and suspicion. We can be born in the likeness of Christ.

To have faith in God is to believe in the powers of overcoming. To paraphrase the words of the Apostle again, "We are afflicted but not crushed; we are cast down, but not destroyed; we are puzzled by a multitude of problems and mysteries, but we are not driven to despair; we are persecuted by the forces of evil, but we are not forsaken. God is working within us. Our physical structure may be weakening, but our souls are full of assurance, courage and hope."

To have faith in God is to believe in the redemptive powers of love—love which compelled Albert Schweitzer to go to an obscure corner in Africa to do his missionary work; love which motivated Frank Laubach to give many of his active years teaching illiterates to read and to write; love which moved a beautiful girl of nobility to become a nurse to bullet-torn bodies, victims of the Second World War; love which inspired man to build temples and shelters; love which convinced Father Flanagan, the builder of Boystown in Nebraska, that there are no hopeless delinquents; love which has redeemed from destruction countless millions of sons and daughters of men; love which bears all things and triumphs over all changes of life.

From God there is no escape. The alternatives are clear: love or perish. Overcome or be destroyed. Begin anew or have no beginning. Say "no" and be condemned; say "yes" and be redeemed.

*God, our ultimate Destiny.*    To have faith in God is to believe that there are powers of judgment at work in history. This judgment is expressed in many ways. Especially is it expressed in instances of national pride, social injustice, exploitation, and the worship of idols. This judgment was operative in ancient Egypt and

Assyria, and it is clearly written upon the walls of our own civilization. As Dr. Herbert Butterfield has said: "Judgment in history falls heaviest on those who think themselves as gods, who fly in the face of providence and history, who put their trust in man-made systems and worship the work of their own hands, who say that the strength of their own right arm gave them the victory."[10]

To have faith in God is to believe in the power of his grace. It is clear that men and nations, even though they may have gone astray, are not eternally condemned. Through their return, rest, and surrender to God, they are and have been healed by the grace of God. Repentant Israel is not the only example.

To have faith in God is to believe in a divine purpose and design. The details of how this design and purpose of God are to be worked out are unknown to us. Assured we can be that there is a purpose, that we are moving toward the fulfillment of His plans.

To have faith in God is to believe in the Kingdom of righteousness. As a space-time realization it may be an impossibility. Yet, to our Christian faith it is the ultimate goal and the ultimate destiny. Whether we deny or affirm this goal, the consequences cannot be escaped.

*Conclusion:* God is alive.

Those who are preoccupied today with the death of God have failed to realize that they are operating with an outmoded, anachronistic, inadequate concept of God. They build a caricature of God and then proceed to show that God is dead. No proof is needed. He never was alive. Their struggle only shows that God is a living reality from whom there is no escape.

## How Important Is Prayer?

*The Text:* "The prayer of a righteous man has great power in its effects" (James 5:16b).

*Introduction:* No excuse for ignorance.

A young person came to me and said: "I do not believe in prayer because I do not think prayers can help." My immediate response to her was this: "It all depends upon what you mean by prayer, what kind of help you are expecting to receive, what you know about the prayer life. It depends upon what you mean by God."

True prayer is never to be identified with a continuous pleading that God would change or break or suspend the laws of His universe. If He were doing this, He would then be turning against himself. As Paul Tillich has said, He would then become demonic—the ground and the power of being fighting against its structure![11]

Authentic prayer is not a continuous effort to persuade God to be loving, kind, gracious, merciful, and forgiving. He is and does this and more, without our persuading.

True prayer is not an autosuggestion or a process of self-deception. For little has a man to suggest to himself when he is faced with tasks greater than he, or when he is in the depth of troubles. Such a man needs to grasp hold of spiritual realities.

Genuine prayer is not intended in any way to be a substitute for planning, study, work, research, or sacrifice. As Paul Johnson has put it, "Prayer is no substitute for action; neither intelligence, trust, or kindness. But action may fail for lack of intelligence. Persons are ill for lack of trust. And poverty is unrelieved without kindness. Prayer is no substitute for a steel chisel or the wind of an airplane. It does not replace muscular action in walking, or faithful study in meeting an examination."[12] Prayer has its own functions to fulfill.

The prayer of an intelligent, righteous man is to be understood in the first place as his thoughts, feelings, aspirations—yea, even the deep and secret desires and *longings of his soul directed Godward.*

It is an act of man's inner search. This kind of prayer is described very beautifully in the 139th Psalm. This prayer is more than mere introspection and self-analysis. It is one's depth research that goes together with a profound longing—"Try me, know me, and lead me in the way everlasting" (See Ps. 139:24). It is self-examination in the light of God's presence—that is, in the spirit of truthfulness, honesty, and sincerity. And this, as Jesus has suggested, often calls for privacy behind closed doors.

True prayer is looking at our innermost souls, with an assurance that "Though the mountains shake and be carried into the midst of the sea, I will not be moved" (Ps. 46). "Nothing will ever separate me from the love of God" (Rom. 8:35–39). "Underneath are the everlasting arms" (Deut. 33:27).

True prayer is an act of rethinking our deepest spiritual needs, knowing that there are sources to satisfy them. Prayer is not an easy, magical, cheap, and swift way of getting everything we want. It is a long-term, patient search, undergirded by undiscourageable faith in God.

When prayer is considered in this light, it then becomes evident that neither work nor recreation; neither study nor scholarship; neither intelligence nor saintliness, kindness, or sacrifice could ever replace it. It has its own functions to fulfill.

***Contact with powers that transcend and transform us.*** "I do not believe in miracles," says Harry Emerson Fosdick, "in the old terms of broken or suspended law, but I have to believe in these scientific miracles, incredible things done by science through releasing of cosmic powers; and I have to believe in personal miracles, incredible things happening in people, to people, for people who have liberated the divine resources."[13]

There are forces of redemption and regeneration available to us. In this realm, prayer means simply fulfilling our inward conditions so that the powers may be released. Prayer is completing the circuit. It means plugging in on a current that is both individual and cosmic—current that gives us light, power, and life.

It is through prayer that our emotional energy is renewed. We are blessed with joy, gladness, exaltation.

It is through prayer that we are released from our tensions. Our worries are dispelled. Our fears are transformed. Our insecurity is overcome. A quiet relaxation, or what the mystics call "orison," is attained.

It is through an intelligent, honest, and sincere prayer that we are liberated from self-deception and illusion. It is through prayer that our souls are awakened to the realities of life. As St. Augustine has put it, "My life shall be real, for it is full of thee, O God."[14]

It is through the prayer of confession and in no other way that we are assured of God's mercy and forgiveness. So very beautifully it is portrayed by the man who said, "God, be merciful to me, a sinner" (Luke 18:13b). He left the temple justified and forgiven, full of gladness and joy.

It is through prayer—that is, through the focusing of our attention on the object of our supreme loyalty—that we become united and integrated within, that we are liberated from powers pulling us in opposite directions.

It is through prayer that we become sensitive to the needs of others, if only we would pray as did St. Francis of Assisi: "Make me a channel, O God!"

It all depends on what we mean by prayer. And so, if it is well understood, we then must agree with the mystics; it is the greatest privilege and the most wonderful opportunity in the world.

***Preparation for creative adventure with God.*** As already implied, prayer is an act of concentration, an act of focusing of our attention on values that are worthy to be enacted beyond our individual lives. The man of God is not, and he cannot be, satisfied with prayers that are concerned with his own well being alone: "God bless my wife, my son, John, and me—us three, and no more; Amen," is not a true prayer. It is a superstitious utterance.

With Abraham, the man of prayer is destined to cry, "Wilt thou indeed destroy the righteous with the wicked? Suppose there are fifty righteous within the city" (Genesis 18:24). With Jesus of Nazareth, he is destined to say: "For their sake I consecrate myself, that they also may be consecrated in truth" (John 17:19).

With God himself, he is destined to brood over the evils, tragedies, sorrows and sufferings of mankind. In deep and profound devotion he is bound to cry, "God, I will not let you go until these my brethren are clothed and fed and liberated from their bondage."

No selfish begging! No illusion, when a poet says,

I ask no dream, no prophet ecstasies,
No sudden rending of the veil of clay,
No angel visitant, no op'ning skies,
But take the dimness of my soul away . . .[15]

*Conclusion:* Called to be a man of prayer.

In 1949, Dr. Albert Schweitzer came to Harvard University. He was invited to play an organ. Here is a testimony of Dean Sperry: "There was not a hint of the virtuoso displaying his talents. Not even the slightest interest was shown as to whether we were listening or not. As he went on he made us feel rather shabby and superficial. You realized he had gone far beyond you into the mysteries of art, music, philosophy, theologies, medicine and life itself.[16]

In his autobiography Schweitzer explains how it all came to be. "It was incomprehensible to me," says he, "even before I went to school, why in my prayers I should pray for human beings only. So, when my mother prayed with me and kissed me goodnight, I used to add silently my own prayers for every living creature. I prayed something like this: 'O Heavenly Father, protect and bless all creatures that have the breath of life. Guard them from evil and let them sleep in peace. Amen.'"[17]

How important is prayer? I cannot even begin to tell. You must experience it for yourself to know. It is the greatest privilege and the greatest opportunity in the world!

## Miracles, Old and New

*The Text:* "A great multitude followed him, because they saw the signs which he did on those who were diseased" (John 6:2).

*Introduction:* False division.

When you talk about miracles, people usually divide themselves into two opposite groups. Some believe in all kinds of miracles; others insist that faith in miracles is sheer superstition.

Some time ago, a young person came to me and said, "I can't believe in miracles. I believe that our world is founded on the laws of nature. In the old days, when people did not know any better, they believed in miracles. They were superstitious. They thought that God could break the laws of nature, that he could make the sun to stand still, an axe head to float on the water. They believed that Jesus could turn water into wine, calm the storm and restore sight to the blind and hearing to the deaf. Today, we know," he said, "such things are impossible."

***Miracles need to be interpreted.*** If all such miracles were to be taken literally, without any deeper meaning, I could not believe them either.

All of the miracle narratives of the Old Testament are not alike. There are some which are merely folklore with little religious significance, if any.

There are miracle narratives in the Bible which seem to be on the borderline. They may puzzle us about their real meaning and significance. "From my point of view," said Harry Emerson Fosdick, "among these narratives are the stories about the miraculous draft of the fishes, the cursing of the fig tree, the casting of the demons into the swine, and the story about Jesus eating a fish after his resurrection." There are several ways to look at them and interpret them.

There are miracle stories in the Bible which are merely expressions of human wonderment and fantasy. There are others, rooted and grounded in history and human experience. The flood narratives, I am sure, were not pulled out of "thin air." Neither were the stories about the escape of the Jewish people from Egypt unrelated to history. The stories about the Israelites in the desert, their conquest of Palestine, their colorful fights for monotheism, were deeply rooted in the facts of history. Yet, their purpose was not to teach history but faith in the greatness and goodness of God.

The question before us is not whether we believe or disbelieve in miracles, but whether we recognize that all kinds of miracle stories are reported in the Holy Scriptures. The question is not whether we do or do not believe that God can break his own natural laws, but whether or not we understand the language or miracle stories and know their deeper meaning.

The time of miracles is not passed.

**We are still surrounded by the miracles of God.** The appearance of life on our little planet, Earth, is an incomprehensible miracle. Scientists may try to explain how all of this took place. The Earth cooled off. The proper conditions developed. Then the elements came together in a wonderful way. Life began in a very simple fashion. From inorganic life developed one-cell organisms. Then, thanks to the evolutionary forces, they produced a more complex life. It still remains a miracle that all of this came to pass.

Even the life of a tomato plant is a miracle. Standing in his garden and looking at his tomato plants, Chad Walsh says: "The sun is pleasantly warm, despite a certain crispness in the air. I know that soon the first frost will blacken my tomato plants, and wilt the wild purple asters growing on the edge of the garden. The sadness that accompanies all endings is salt to my tomato. How transient the life of a tomato plant is and how many gifts in combination it is dependent: soil, water, sun, warmth, an atmosphere free of poisons—and my own willingness to plant and hoe and fertilize.

"It seems presumptuous to hope that next year all these gifts will exist in the right combination. When frost makes its first onslaught,

the idea of another spring will be a sheer act of faith, resting in confidence that God is both loving and reliable.

"Again, I look at the seed. Locked inside of it is perhaps a billion
years of living history and a plant that wants to climb toward the
sun. I doubt that God will disappoint it."[18]

The birth of a baby, the growth and the development of the human
brain often have been accepted as common occurrences. Yet, when
we think of the intricacies of the human body, the purposiveness of
all of the glands, the muscles, and the nerve cells, how can one help
but wonder and wonder again?

At the end of the *Larousse Encyclopedia of Astronomy* we read:
"Thanks to Astronomy, the inquiring spirit of man has at last discovered the true status of humanity in the universe: a mere atom,
but a thinking atom, situated on a microscopic planet, one of several
revolving about a small and commonplace star, itself indistinguish-
able from a hundred thousand others, in the heart of a galaxy which
in turn is lost among the millions and millions that populate the
tiny corner of space that we have been able to explore."[19] Only a
little atom, yet able to explore and to begin to understand the
mysteries of God's universe! What wonderment beyond words! Only
a little atom in God's endless universe, yet able to experience the
beauty, wisdom, goodness, and the love of God! Able to dream the
dreams of God! Hopeful to build God's kingdom on earth.

*Conclusion:* Called To Promote God's Mighty Acts.

Our task is not so much to speculate as to act. Contemporary
miracles depend upon our cooperation with God. He has chosen
you and me to lead the exodus, to provide shelter in wilderness, to
still the storms and heal the sick. Bernie Warfield is a shining example.[20] And you can be an example too.

## Watch Out, Its Fire Is Real!

*The* Text: "And if your hand causes you to sin, cut it off; it is better
for you to enter life maimed than with two hands to go to hell, to the
unquenchable fire . . . where their worm does not die, and the
fire is not quenched" (Mark 9:43, 48).

*Introduction:* The Valley Hinnom

Outside of Jerusalem there is a valley which in the distant past belonged to a man called Hinnom. Here, in the early days of Jewish history, idolaters used to sacrifice their children to Moloch (II Chronicles 28:3).

After the Deuteronomic reformation, the Valley of Hinnom was regarded as an accursed place. Everything useless and unclean was thrown into it to be burned. It thus became a city dump.

Jesus knew the Valley of Hinnom. And so, when he wanted to describe an inward fire, he turned to an outward picture which was familiar to all of his listeners.

**Self-condemnation is hell.** In the city dump there are no values to be found. There are no meaningful relationships of any kind. As someone else has said it, "A skeleton here does not belong to a tin can, and a tin can does not belong to a skeleton." It is a place where the smoke continues and the fires are not put out. It is the dirtiest place on earth.

In the Scriptures we read, "There was a rich man, who was clothed in purple and fine linen and who feasted sumptuously every day. And at his gate lay a poor man named Lazarus, full of sores, who desired to be fed with what fell from the rich man's table; moreover the dogs came and licked his sores" (Luke 16:19–21).

It never occurred to the rich man that Lazarus was also a human being. He, too, had human feelings. He, also, had his needs. He, too, was entitled to life, liberty, and the pursuit of happiness. The rich man was a fool. His eyes were blind; his ears were deaf; his heart was totally selfish. He had no sense of human solidarity.

At the end of his life, when he realized that he had lived in total selfishness, that he belonged to no one, and no one belonged to him, he was tragically oppressed by a feeling of being thrown into a city dump, "where the worm does not die, and the fire is not quenched."

To experience a feeling of belonging to no one, a feeling of being a tin can in a city dump, one does not have to die; for, wherever selfishness is triumphant over love and concern for others, hell is already there in all its potentiality.[21] I saw its reality almost beyond endurance during World War II.

I will never forget the words of a man who came to see me some time ago and began his tragic story saying, "Dear Pastor, I belong to no one and no one belongs to me." The mist of hell had already filled the soul of our visiting friend. Already, he was there "where the worm does not die, and the fire is not quenched."

*Hell is a realization that life has been wasted.*  At the end of man's life it is hard to imagine anything more tragic than this confession: "My life is finished. No battles have I fought; no victories have I won; no values have I promoted; no dreams have I dreamt; no heritage have I to leave behind. My life has been a total waste." He is already in the midst of hell, even before his journey is finished.

According to the picture of the last judgment, recorded in Luke, those who were standing on the left-hand side of Christ were shocked by his words: "Depart, ye cursed." In their lifetime they had not been aware of any waste or any misuse of their time, their talent, their treasures, and their opportunities. In great surprise they turned to Jesus and said, "When did we see you hungry or thirsty or naked, or in prison and did not minister unto you?" (Matthew 25:44). No sooner was the question finished when their consciences began to speak. Opportunities they had had; yet, all of them had been wasted.

The parable which Jesus told about the talents may seem to imply a rather ruthless, harsh, and oversevere judgment. The man who had not made any use of his talent, one which he had saved to return to his Master, was ordered to be thrown into the utmost darkness of hell. Outwardly, the man had not done anything wrong. He had just wanted to play safe. Can you blame him? After all, he had only one talent. You don't gamble with just one talent, do you? Yet, Jesus sent him into the depths of hell, for even that one talent which he had received, had been wasted. He had made no use of it.

Or, think for a moment about the fig tree. Remember, Jesus cursed it. He did it because there were no fruits to be found on the tree. He did it, I believe, to demonstrate that every life which bears no fruit, every life which is lived in a vacuum—in emptiness—is an accursed life.

Hell is a realization of emptiness, a feeling of meaninglessness, and an awareness that life has been wasted, that all opportunities have gone. Such punishing awareness was expressed by a man who had lived only to receive and who had given nothing. These are his words: "I could have lived a different life: I could have been a different man; I could have given my life for a cause. This I have not done—my life has been totally wasted." Here is a taste of being thrown into the city dump, "where the worm does not die, and the

fire is not quenched." Here is a foretaste of being thrown into the
fires of an inward hell.

According to Jesus, the Valley of Hinnom was only an outward
picture of hell. Real hell to him meant an inward experience of fear,
dread, and condemnation, anchored in an expectation of *destruction
as the ultimate end of life*.

Evidently such feelings do not come out of the blue sky. At the end
of one's journey, they presuppose a life that has been lived in separation from God. They are a testimony to a lifelong rebellion against
God and his kingdom—a rebellion against whatever is true, lovely,
beautiful, and praiseworthy. They presuppose a religion that is
based on an illusion—an expectation of the crown of life without any
sacrifice, any self-giving. They are the result of a meaningless and
purposeless living—a waste of time, talent, and possessions. They
stem from total unrelatedness to God, Christ, and one's fellow man.[22]

God has not destined us to live in a city dump. The choice is always our own. Lazarus is always here to remind us: Relate yourself
to the needs of others.

There is a road that leads to hell. There is also a road that leads
to meaningful being. Which road we take depends upon the decisions we make today, tomorrow, and in the faraway future.

*Conclusion:* Radical are the demands of Jesus, but they are redemptive.

If you want to save your life, you must be willing to give it in
a fashion of Christian extravagance. "If your hand causes you to
sin, cut it off." Don't play around with the temptation of self-
centered living. "It is better for you to enter life maimed than with
two hands to go to hell, to the unquenchable fire . . . where their
worm does not die, and the fire is not quenched."

## An Evidence of Life Eternal

*The Text:* "And this is eternal life, that they know thee the only
true God, and Jesus Christ whom thou hast sent" (John 17:3).

*Introduction:* Eternal life has been interpreted in many ways.

For primitive men, eternal life meant shadowy existence beyond
a grave. According to their precepts, when life on earth is finished,
it continues in the world beneath—very much in the same fashion

as it does here. Farmers are farmers still; poets are busy with their poetry; soldiers are ready for warfare. The dead carpenters still need their tools; the dead warriors—their weapons; the departed souls still need their nourishment. To us, such a belief in immortality is out of the question.

As time went on, and Christianity came upon the scene, a belief developed that life after death is not a shadowy existence but is, rather, an existence far more beautiful than anything we have dreamt, imagined, or encountered. The expectation was a hopeful one; there will be no suffering, no pain, no troubles, no hardships and crises, no separation from loved ones, no sin and no separation from God.

In the nineteenth century another idea was explored: "Nothing that is shall perish utterly, but perish only to revive again."[23]

The Orientals have spoken about immortality of words, worth, and works. Some have called this an aristocratic view. "What we need," says Ashley Montague, "is a belief that everyone is immortal in the sense that whatever men do lives on somehow, somewhere, and somewhen ... There is an immortality of the evil that men do as well as the good they do, of the vulgar as well as of the sublime, of the ugly as well as the beautiful, of stupidity as well as wisdom, of selfishness as well as service, the immortality, in short, of what one is."[24]

Such a view may be widely accepted. Yet, eternal life is not living on "somewhere, somehow, somewhen." It is *an awareness and knowledge of God.*

Eternal life is not a matter of craving for an existence beyond the grave, however beautiful and rewarding that existence may be. To be sure, as long as we are in our bodily form, we must "suffer and groan" and long for a heavenly liberation. Yet, eternal life itself is not a contrast between now and then or here and there.

Eternal life is a present reality in the sense that a mature Christian may walk with joy and confidence, knowing that he lives and moves and has his being in God. It is God's own truth that illumines him, God's own love that unfolds him, God's own power that strengthens him, God's eternal arms and goodness that uphold him. It is God's own grace that redeems him from destruction and will crown him with rewards beyond his expectation.

Eternal life is a present reality within the soul of the believer who knows that nothing can ever separate him from the love of God, manifested in the life of Christ.

Eternal life is a present reality as a new understanding of life, death, and a new outlook on values.

Eternal life is a present vision of the depth and the breadth and the height of life. To paraphrase our text: Your knowledge of God, your knowledge which is very intimate and personal is your evidence of life eternal, already present and much more to come.

Eternal life, according to our text is *power and courage to be.*

To Paul, John, and others, the Risen Christ did not mean a post-mortem physical structure. It meant power to affirm their existence and power to overcome the forces of "this world."

What convinced the disciples of the resurrection and eternal life of Christ was not the empty tomb. It was the experience of the power of God, which they had seen in Christ before, and which now was within their own souls, that persuaded them that Christ had risen indeed and was alive.

Previous to this experience, all of them had failed miserably to stand up for their Master. After the crucifixion, all of them had gone into hiding. All of them had made many terrible blunders. How long this deadly existence continued we do not know. Yet, the day of miracle did come. They were transformed and ready to transform others.

Eternal life is the power of God in everyday living. And the only real evidence of this life eternal is to be found in a profound, true, personal experience with God in the most down-to-earth matters.

Eternal life is *living in a vicarious fashion.*

Only God is unconditionally eternal. We can hope to share eternal life with him only to the extent to which we have a part in his plans, in his purposes, in his spirit. All else in the world is finite, perishable, mortal, subject to non-being.

It was God's own dreams which Jesus dreamt. It was God's kingship he proclaimed. For it he lived and suffered and died. It was God's everlasting arms into which he committed his spirit as he finished his pilgrimage. It was the power of God in which he participated and it enabled him to triumph over the forces of death and destruction, which lifted him on the level of life everlasting.

So often we complain that the world is full of troubles. In a self-complacent and self-righteous attitude we say, "Why should it be so if God is in charge of this world? Why doesn't he take care of his own?" We look at these problems and forget that these may be our only real opportunities to live in a vicarious fashion.

*Conclusion:* Invited to Eternal Life.

We probably will never become as saintly as was St. Francis of Assisi; yet, all of us could pray as he did, and much of our life would be changed.

*The angel of Elyne.*[25] The church and the village of Elyne had been destroyed. For a long time, both had been in mournful ruins. Selfish egotism had gone so far that no one had cared for the rebuilding of the house of worship. Then something miraculous happened. The village blacksmith discovered that many a decorative piece from the church, now in ruins, had been stolen and built into a pigsty! He summoned every villager to witness what "man had done." When their indignation was at its highest, he led them to the place where the church used to be and showed what God had done with rain and sun and the spring flowers. New life was born now also in the souls of men.

## CHAPTER SEVEN

# WRESTLING With COMMUNITY PROBLEMS

As ministers of the gospel, we are obligated to preach on controversial issues of our society. We need not pretend that we have "all the answers" for we do not possess such wisdom. Our task is rather to relate our Christian faith to the issues of contemporary society and thereby enact the prayer of Jesus: "Thy kingdom come; thy will be done on earth as it is in heaven." The gospel is always relevant to human life. It is our task to interpret and relate it. Our success or failure in doing this depends largely upon the way we approach our problems. Here are some of the areas which are of deep concern to our parishioners: (1) Christian citizenship; (2) dangers of communism; (3) racial and cultural crises; (4) poverty in the land of plenty; (5) competition and covetousness; (6) Christian unity.

Following are outlines and short excerpts of sermons preached on Christian social issues.

## Allies or Enemies of God?

*The Text:* "Only take care lest this liberty of yours somehow become a stumbling-block to the weak" (I Cor. 8:9).

*Introduction:* Two kinds of Americans.

A statement that all Americans are either allies or enemies of God would be as silly as the one that the moon is made of green cheese. There are Americans that are "as good as gold," who would be willing to go not only the second but also the third mile to help their fellow men in need.

There are others, however, whose highest good is nothing more than power, wealth, and success, who would not hesitate to exploit even the noblest principles of religion for selfish gains. Americans they still are; yet, by no stretch of the imagination could they be claimed as God's allies.

There are noble Americans who are dedicated to the progress of knowledge, the promotion of justice, and the realization of human brotherhood. Yet, there are others, unfortunately, who are narrow nationalists and racists, who are irreligious as any communist in the Red Square in Moscow. Tragically enough, Americans they all are; yet, clearly they are not on God's side, for we are on his side only when we are for *liberty with responsibility*.

Liberty has often been understood merely as freedom of thought, freedom of expression, and freedom of action. Without these, no one is a sovereign, independent, and autonomous being; without these, no one is a full citizen. Yet, when liberty encompasses nothing more than a demand for such rights for one's self alone, it is not a true liberty. As Merimon Cuninggim has put it, "If any man demands such rights for himself alone, he means not to live in a free society but to be the governor in an enslaved society."[1]

Only that liberty is truly sweet which is concerned with the well-being of all; or, as it has been put in the Preamble to the Constitution, which is concerned with the promotion of the general welfare of the people. We are on God's side only when we are for *liberty rooted in justice*.

At a superficial glance, justice may seem to be an easy requirement. Yet, when we begin to think of it in terms of concrete life situations, it then presents to us a profound problem.

Today, God does not come to us in a recognizable fashion. He comes to us with the needs of the world, the needs of the hungry, thirsty, and the sick. He comes to us with the needs of the underprivileged and uneducated, the needs of the sin-sick world to whom the church is called to minister. For an illustration I refer you to a story told by Leo Tolstoy about a shoemaker's dream.

One night a cobbler dreamt that the next day Christ was coming to his shop. He got up early in the morning and decorated his shop so that it would be appropriate to receive such a great guest. He waited all morning, and no one came except an old man, asking to rest. The cobbler saw that his shoes were thoroughly worn out, so while the old man rested, the shoemaker fashioned a pair of shoes for him and sent him on his way.

He waited again through the afternoon, and the only person who appeared was an old woman, tired and hungry. Out of his compassion, the cobbler gave her some food. She ate it with relish and, refreshed, went on her way.

When the shades of night began to fall, there came into his shop a lost child, crying bitterly. The shoemaker was quite annoyed but could not refuse to help the child, and showed him the way to his home.

When he returned, he fell on his knees and prayed saying, "Why is it, Lord, that your feet delay? Have you forgotten that this was the day?" Then, softly in the silence he heard a voice: "Lift up your heart for I kept my word. Three times I came to your friendly door; three times my shadow was on your floor. I was the beggar with bruised feet; I was the woman you gave to eat; I was the child on the homeless street."

We are on God's side when we stand for *liberty with religious maturity*.

Religious neutrality is not only absurd, it is unthinkable. Our ultimate issue is not God or no God, but what kind of ultimate concern is in accordance with reason and love. When the God of wisdom, love, and law is dethroned, the God of ignorance, provincialism, and chaos will surely take his seat.

In our pluralistic culture, there is a great deal of confusion in the area of ethics and moral values. There are individuals who sincerely believe that every ethical principle is relative, that all ethical norms are subject to change.

There are others who sincerely believe that all ethical norms, propositions, and conclusions are absolute, and that they do not change according to time, place, persons, and interests.

From the point of view of our Christian gospel, neither orientation is fully adequate. If all ethical principles and norms were relative, then by this very fact they would cease to be even relative. They would have no rational foundation. By the same token, if all ethical norms, propositions and judgments were declared as absolute, we would have to close our eyes to the facts of life and declare ourselves equal with God, perfect in wisdom, power, and love.

The truth of the gospel is that only God-given imperatives are absolute. Our own interpretations are always relative. It **would be** sheer arrogance, egotism, and ignorance to claim that our particular ethical judgments and conclusions were as absolute as the norms of God. And so, if there is to be tolerance, compromise, harmony, and cooperation in our land, we need to recognize our imperfections while we proclaim the absolute perfection of God.

True liberty rests upon our recognition of goals and purposes which transcend our personal, family, and national interests. True liberty is always tied together with an outgoing orientation.

Apostle Paul did not compose his hymn of love for Jews or Christians alone, but for the citizens of the world who speak in many tongues, accents, and dialects. He wrote it because he knew that without this other-love, religion is an opiate for the people; without it, politics is persecution, education is the training of animals, industry is exploitation, business is covered-up burglary and corruption.

When the Pilgrim fathers landed on our shores in 1620, they signed a covenant which recognized this responsibility. It was not an accident that 313 years later on March 4, 1933—after a dreadful plague of national depression—in his First Inaugural Address, President Franklin Delano Roosevelt declared, "We are not stricken by a plague of locusts. Plenty is still at our doorstep. Only the generous use of it languishes because the rulers of exchange of mankind's goods have failed . . . The money changers have fled from their high seats in the temple of civilization. Now we may restore the temple to an ancient truth . . . These dark days will be worth all they cost us if they teach us that our true destiny is not to be ministered unto but to minister to ourselves and to our fellow men."[2]
*Conclusion:* Called to be God's allies.

There is a story told by Dr. Elton Trueblood about a Negro and a white man who were looking for a room in one of New York's hotels. The Negro had just been refused, the clerk's reason being "no vacancy." Shortly thereafter, the white man turned to the clerk and asked the same. The answer was, "What price did you have in mind?" After the white man was assured that he could have a room in the hotel, he turned to the Negro and said, "Come back; the clerk has made a mistake. There is a room for you because there is a room for me!" Then, turning to the clerk, the white man said, "And what are you going to do about it? You know the law.

I mean to see that this law is enforced." Undoubtedly, he was one of God's allies, for he stood for liberty with a sense of responsibility, justice, and outgoing concern.

## Our Answer to Communism

*The Text:* "For we are not contending against flesh and blood, but against principalities, against the powers, against the world rulers of this present darkness, against the spiritual hosts of wickedness in the heavenly places" (Eph. 6:12).

*Introduction:* The beginnings of communism.

Communism, which now is a political, economic, and religious dictatorship, was introduced by Karl Marx and Frederick Engels. The aims of both of these men were to provide answers to the problems of poverty, war, exploitation, and superstition. And let it be understood, they were not fighting imagined, nonexisting evils. There was exploitation, corruption, oppression. All kinds of superstitious beliefs and practices were proclaimed as good faith in the name of God and the church.

Because of the half-truth[3] that this movement contains, it grew by leaps and bounds and became established in the Soviet Union, in the vast territory of China, and in many other lands. In order to block their expansion and their destructive work, we ought to know *the communist creed.*

Communism is not identical with socialism—there is a distinct difference between Marxian Communism and, let us say, Guild Socialism, Fabian Socialism, Cooperative Socialism, and Christian Socialism.

The communist creed asserts that religion is an opiate for the people, and thus, it ought to be abolished.[4] Let no one deceive us. Communists are hard at work, both day and night, to bring about their dream. To discredit religion, they have used every psychological principle known. By means of official prayers, slogans, posters, legislative powers, schools, university teachers and professors, they have been and are continuously fighting religion in all areas of life.

In the Soviet Union the church is living, to a large extent, by the grace of the state. It is subject to the whims and the wishes of the atheistic government. Many of the theological seminaries have been closed. Leaders of the various denominations have been forced to bow before the authorities. The freedom of the preachers to speak on all of the social issues has been taken away. Taken away also has been the freedom of the people to attend church services without fear of repercussions.

The communist creed asserts that all private property ought to be abolished.[5] To them, private property is the source of almost all evils. It is responsible for greed, hate, and class struggle; for prejudice, exploitation, and oppression. According to the communist government, therefore, all farms, industries, banks, health and welfare organizations, educational institutions, even private homes of more than three or four rooms ought to be owned and operated by the communist government. Accordingly, when the Soviet government took over our native Latvia, wholesale confiscation of all kinds took place in the name of justice and humanity. No one should be so naïve as to believe that an abolition of all private property would free our society and its individuals from all evils. Yet, a dogmatic communist is destined to swear on this belief.

The communist creed asserts that the existing world order should also be abolished.[6] Communists consider our democracy a sham because (in their opinion) the owners of large properties have greater power than the rest of the people. Our capitalistic system, from their viewpoint, is so corrupt that there can never be real freedom, justice, and love. It has to be abolished. To accomplish this, they have a multitude of spies, informers, and saboteurs at work all around the globe. And we dare not forget that a dedicated communist is ready to crawl on his naked belly over ice and snow and sand to fulfill his "sacred" mission.[7]

The communist creed asserts that any means may be used to achieve their ultimate goal—world domination. The Manifesto says that the communists believe in the establishment of the proletarian dictatorship by means of force, violence, bloodshed, and revolutions.[8]

If we are to fight communism, we ought to know its positive errors as well as its half-truths. To fight communism successfully, we need to know *the communist language*.

When communists speak about free elections and democratic government, they do not mean the same as we do. Although it is true that almost 100 percent of the people participate in any one Soviet election, we ought to know that they do so because there is no choice. They are compelled to cast their ballots. The alternative is to starve, suffer, and die, possibly in the white forests of Siberia. The communists do not understand peaceful co-existence as we do. To the communists, co-existence is a means toward their goal of world domination.

When communists speak about classless society, they do not mean an integrated society, nor even a one-class society whereby all are absolutely alike. They stand for society in which the dominating factor is the proletariat.

When communists talk about the worth of an individual human being they are quite hypocritical. Basically, in the Soviet system an individual has only an instrumental value. He is valuable only to the extent to which he can render service to the communist cause.

Freedom in communist language has a very special connotation. To the communists freedom means governmental power to demand absolute obedience. Complete religious, economic, political, and intellectual freedoms as we understand them are nonexistent in the Soviet Union. And it is quite unlikely that by means of tyranny they will finally arrive at freedom worthy of its name.

Communist leaders are anxious to persuade us that they are dedicated to promote world peace—meaning, undoubtedly, peace under the flag of hammer and sickle. Under Premier Khrushchev, mass murders and unspeakable brutalities, which communists committed during the Stalin regime, apparently have been discontinued. Yet, the "hate song" of the young pioneer is still very much alive. By no stretch of the imagination can it be called the song of peace.

***Communist expansion can be blocked.***   We are doing it when we promote a religion that is free from superstitious relics and meaningless clichés and phraseology. We are doing it when we unmask the people who are indirectly supporting the communist cause by accusing our church leaders of being pro-communistic.

We are blocking communist expansion when we disclose the motivatiton of those who keep on shouting, "Suppress every socially constructive enterprise! Suppress every kind of progress! Oppose integration! Keep everything the same as it was years and years ago!" As Herman Reissig has said, "Whoever helps to stop racial discrimination, helps to stop communism. Whoever works for justice, works against communism. Whoever helps to eliminate corruption in business, in labor unions, in government, helps to overcome communism. Whoever works for good laws and their enforcement, whoever takes seriously his responsibilities in public life, whoever resists temptations to cheat his fellow citizen or his government, whoever supports civil liberties is striking blows against international communism."[9]

*Conclusion:* Dedicated to nobler ideas.

The time has not come for us to abolish all armaments. To do that would be a clear invitation for communists to take over. Yet, we must remember that in the final analysis, communism will not be defeated by swords and guns, but by ideas that are better than theirs and by people that are fully committed to the enactment of these ideas in life.

The strategy of dictatorship we propose to meet with the strategy of democracy. The strategy of oppression and exploitation we propose to meet with freedom, justice, and concern. The strategy of hate we propose to meet with the strategy of love. The communist religion with its own opiate for the people we propose to meet with a religion of realism, truth, and maturity. The day will come when even the communists will see that faith is truer than doubt. A neighbor is better than a spy. And love is stronger than hate.

## Poverty in the Land of Plenty

*The Text:* "Has not God chosen those who are poor in the world to be rich in faith and heirs of the kingdom which he has promised to those who love him?" (James 2:5).

*Introduction:* Poverty and plenty.

Ours is an affluent society. Yet, we know that in our midst there are evidences of a continuing massive poverty. According to the statistics provided by the National Council of Churches of Christ, poverty engulfs more than 50,000,000 Americans. To all who believe in an applied gospel, poverty is a religious issue. And yet, many times it has been *viewed as a source of blessing*.

The gospels are full of illustrations where poor people are praised and the wealthy, criticized. Think, if you would, about the parable concerning the rich man and the poor Lazarus, or the illustration about the rich young ruler who came to Jesus wishing to be his disciple but because of his selfishness and his great wealth could not do it. Or think, for the sake of contrast, about the poor widow who brought an offering larger than a tithe to the temple. She gave her all. Clearly, in all such cases Jesus was siding with the poor.

The disciples of Jesus were poor people. Yet, they were called to a wonderful mission. Speaking about himself and the early followers of Christ, Apostle Paul is reported to have said, "Consider your call, brethren; not many of you were wise according to worldly standards, not many were powerful, not many were of noble birth" (I Cor. 1:26). Evidently he believed that the poor are especially fitted to do the work of Christ.

It is a fact that many of the scientists, scholars, reformers, artists, composers, and religious leaders have been people who have been intimately acquainted with the meaning of poverty. For many, the pressures of poverty have closed the gates of boredom, licentiousness, and destruction, and have opened the portals of the kingdom of God.

Yet, there is another way of looking at human poverty. It is evident that *continuous poverty is a curse.*

We were coming from our vacation in New Hampshire. Our route went through a slum area in New York City. Some rain had fallen a few hours before, but not enough to wash the dirt from the streets. Many children were playing in the middle of the busy thoroughfare. Every inch around them spoke of poverty, want, and deprivation. As we were driving on I thought of a little boy who kept pushing his play cart continuously into the busy traffic. I wondered what would become of this young man when he grew up. Would he accept the poverty that surrounded him as a challenge and become, like Irving Berlin, a great creative spirit in the world of music, or would he become a delinquent, a criminal, a drug addict like the one who has said: "Heroin is my shepherd."[10]

Heroin is my shepherd. I shall always want.
It maketh me to lie down in gutters. It leadeth me beside
    still madness. It destroyeth my soul.
It leadeth me in the paths of hell for its name's sake.
Yea, though I walk through the valley of the shadow of death,

I will fear no evil, for heroin art with me. My syringe and
spike shall comfort me.
Thou puttest me to shame in the presence of mine enemies.
Thou anointest my head with madness.
My cup runneth over with sorrow.
Surely hate and evil shall follow me all the days of my life,
And I will dwell in the house of misery and disgrace for ever.[10]

There is a point at which economic hardships cease to be a stimu-
lus and a challenge and become a source of injury and destruction.
In a great many cases poverty has led its victims to personal destruction, to resentment, rebellion, frustration, a broken spirit, anti-
social attitudes, and all kinds of personally destructive acts.

Poverty is destructive not only of personal life, but of family life
as well. Many families have been torn asunder by the lack of sufficient means of livelihood. Many a tension and argument in family living has been caused by economic burdens; desertion, de-
linquency, illegitimacy, and sex degradation have often been found
together with strong pressures of poverty.

Directly or indirectly, poverty has often led to serious troubles on
the levels of community and national life. Group conflicts, chasms,
segregation, and an ever-increasing expenditure of money to combat
the crimes that are rooted in poverty have weakened our national
spirit, unity, national strength, and defenses.

Temporary poverty may be a blessing. Yet, persistent poverty in
an affluent society is a curse no church can bless or sanction, no
Christian can afford to look at with indifference or satisfaction.

*We are called to abolish poverty.* According to statistics,
ours is one of the wealthiest communities in the land. Yet, across
the tracks we have a large slum area. There are houses unfit for
human dwelling. There are streets that need to be paved. There are
families that live on substandard income. With your interest and
mine, much could be done to change this situation. Old houses
could be torn down and replaced. Streets could be paved. Our Negro
families could be provided with planned parenthood information.
All of this is within the realm of an immediate possibility.

It goes without saying that we need equal protection for all
workers under labor legislation, including minimum wages, unem-
ployment insurance, and workmen's compensation. Yet, there is

much more we can do in our community to encourage our people across the tracks to improve their economic status. Many of them have talents which have been neglected simply because these individuals believe that only limited areas of job opportunities are open to them. It is up to us to see that no truly qualified person be denied a job simply because of his race, creed, or national origin.

Much of the poverty across the tracks in our own community, however, is determined by a lack of adequate education and vocational training. In his *Strategy for Peace*, our late President, John Fitzgerald Kennedy, has made this observation: "We have been assuming that our superior wealth would obtain a superior education for our children. But we have failed to devote more than a tiny fraction—at most three per cent—of our national income for this purpose, as contrasted to the Soviet's ten per cent."[11] Now, when it comes to the money we have spent in our community for the education of underprivileged children, I am afraid that all of us would be ashamed of the figure.

Our federal government alone cannot abolish poverty. Much of the work needs to be done by Christian citizens. We can promote education, fair employment practices, and slum clearances in our own town and thus provide an example for others.

*Conclusion:* Let me paraphrase the text.

Blessed are the poor, who, by their own poverty, have been challenged to work and labor with love and devotion for a richer and fuller life. Blessed are those who, although they have never been poor, are dedicated to the task of liberating man from the curse of poverty. And blessed is the church that believes in sharing its wealth, physical and spiritual, in order that people everywhere may know the liberating truth of the gospel.

## Reconciled and Integrated

*The Text:* "The aim of our charge is love that issues from a pure heart . . ." (I Tim. 1:5).

*Introduction:* Believers in love.

All of us are firm believers in Christian love, brotherhood, and integration. We know the commandments of God: "You shall love the Lord your God with all your heart, with all your soul, with all your mind, and with all your strength . . . and your neighbor as yourself. There is no other commandment greater than these" (Mark 12:30, 31).

It is clear to all of us also that the law of our land is deeply anchored in the same religious orientation. The importance of brotherly love and respect is well affirmed in this excerpt from the Declaration of Independence: "We hold these truths to be self-evident; that all men are created equal, and are endowed by their Creator with certain inalienable rights, among which are life, liberty, and the pursuit of happiness."

*We know that segregation is evil.* We need not be told that racial, national, and denominational hatred serves no constructive purpose. Hatred, we know, is poison not only in our own blood stream; it is poison also in human relations. It is destructive of human welfare, human life, and social order.

At the base of segregation and racial discrimination is nothing positive; at the base of it are pride and prejudice, hate and ignorance, sin and selfishness. The other day a woman called me and said, "I have discovered something and I am amazed! I have just learned that in two months' time some of the primitive people of Africa acquired the ability to use our very complex machinery and some of our very advanced techniques. I can hardly believe this to be possible!"

I said to her, "It is amazing, indeed, how much faster they can acquire new knowledge than many of us can. It is amazing how much stronger their motivation for learning is than that of many of our young people. I am sure that given equal opportunities with us, they would produce as many scholars, scientists, and philosophers as any other race." All this we know only too well; yet, *our problems of segregation persist.*

The whole world knows that many of our colleges and institutions of higher learning, both in the North and in the South, are not yet fully integrated. The whole world knows our tragedy in Mississippi, where millions of dollars have been spent to enforce the law of the land, where battalions of our National Guard have been called out to guarantee the security of one Negro boy wanting to get his education at the University of Mississippi. All of this in our "sweet land of liberty"!

It is so amazing that while we claim that lack of education, ignorance, and stupidity are the real barriers to integration, at the same time we keep the doors of many of our educational institutions closed to these children so anxious, so extremely anxious to learn.

The whole world knows that many of our churches are not as integrated as they ought to be. I am sure that it is not true that none of our fine, professional, educated Negro families would want to be in our company. I have a reason for saying this. Last year, without fanfare or publicity, we integrated our Ministerial Association. There were several doubting Thomases who said, "Don't waste your time; they won't come." Twelve months have passed. Our Negro ministers have been most faithful in their attendance—more reliable, in fact, than some of our own "big" brothers. With tears in their eyes they have told me how happy they are to have this privilege of being in the same Ministerial Association as all other ministers in Winter Park.

The whole world knows, we are not as integrated as we ought to be in areas of employment, housing, transportation, recreation, and entertainment. I am glad to say that there are many signs of progress. Yet, we are moving altogether too slowly. How strange! Negroes can serve in our finest restaurants, prepare food for our families, take care of our little ones; yet, they do not dare to have a part at our table fellowship, nor do they dare to live next door to us.

Behind these problems are many reasons. Some are very old traditions; others are economic concerns; still others are unhappy experiences in the past. Our basic problem, however, is *reconciliation with God.*

Insofar as integration is a matter of outward behavior, it can be legislated, ordered, compelled, and enforced. Insofar as it is a matter of love, out of a pure heart, no outside force could even begin to bring it about. It presupposes an educated and an integrated self.

Even the finest channels of Christian saints can become blocked and narrowed by worldly cares, anxieties, fears, and anxious craving. It is so easy to use people and enjoy things rather than enjoy people and use things. If there is to be any real integration, our spiritual channels need to be cleaned; our communication with God, reestablished; our values, reevaluated.

We need to put ourselves in the shoes of our Negro brethren and say, "How would I feel if one beautiful morning I found myself on the other side of the tracks? How would I feel if one day I saw myself with black skin? How would I act toward others? How would I want others to act toward me?" Use your imagination!

We need to remember that God's love toward us is inseparably bound together with our love toward others. Our feelings are their feelings. Our needs are their needs. Our hopes are their hopes. Our God is their God.

*Conclusion:* A call to practical love, not violence.

This is not a call to an unrealistic appraisal of our differences—economical, social, and educational. At the present time, many such differences exist. This is not a call to emotionalism of any kind—emotionalism issuing in an outburst of shallow slogans of brotherhood. This is an appeal to reason, sound judgment, maturity and Christian love.

It is a joy to relate that in our church, during the past year, we have provided a scholarship for a fine Negro girl. We know she is doing well in her studies. The reports are most encouraging and satisfying. How wonderful it would be if every church in the United States were doing the same. There are a thousand other practical "projects" we can undertake. If these were enacted, motivated by love out of a pure heart, segregation would soon be conquered!

## Covetousness and Competition

*The Text:* "You shall not covet . . ." (Exodus 20:17).

*Introduction:* Covetousness exemplified.

Long ago, we are told by Aesop, Zeus summoned his citizens and said to one of them, "I will give you anything your heart desires. The only condition is that you tolerate someone else having twice as much of anything as you have. If you do not fulfill this condition, you will lose one eye." Immediately, the man responded saying, "I am willing that you take one of my eyes right away. I know I will feel greedy toward those who have twice as much of everything as I have." He lost his eye.

**Covetousness defined.** Covetousness hardly needs a definition. It is that burning passion within us which pushes us to outdo, outsmart, outshine all others. It is that feeling which prohibits us from appreciating the achievements of others. It is that little voice within us which, when it observes others making a fortune, others being cited for services or being elected to an office, says, "Why could not I have done it all?"

According to the Scriptures, covetousness is a deadly sin because it breeds many others. It is a source of many troubles: heartaches, high blood pressure, nervous tensions, breakdown, sorrows, and suffering. It has pushed many a person into the grave long before his destined time. It means enmity with God, Christ, and society. It also means enmity within our own souls (Psalm 10:3; Hab. 2:9; I Cor. 6:10).

***Covetousness and its outreach.***   According to Karl Marx, the source of all kinds of misery is to be found in the economic system of private property, free enterprise, and the capitalist way of production. Says Marx, "Accumulation of wealth at one pole is, therefore, at the same time accumulation of misery, agony, toil, slavery, ignorance, brutality and mental degradation at the opposite pole."[12] "This accumulation," he continues, "plays in political economy about the same part as original sin in theology."[13] From his viewpoint, capitalists are doomed to live in envy, greed, covetousness, and struggle.

No one would argue with Marx that covetousness has many opportunities in a society of free enterprise and private property. No one would deny that in a free society there are many people who are blinded by covetous feelings and in their blindness are reaching for the status of others—their luxury homes, their cars, their bank accounts.

Undoubtedly, covetousness is a sin of our culture. There are many possessions one may covet and aspire to obtain in a negative fashion in the society of plenty. Yet, it is an error to believe that the basic source of covetousness is in the system itself or in private property. Covetousness is not an attribute of property or of a system of production. It may flourish equally well in any society, in any system.

The many instances of human misery, exploitation, and human degradation which Marx has observed in the capitalist society can easily be discovered also in the Soviet system.[14]

Covetousness lives on even where all private property is abolished. It lives on even where the state is claimed to be the owner of everything—even where the goal is said to be, "from each according to his ability and to each according to his need." A person may covet not only another person's possessions, but also his political power, his social status, and his reputation. A person may covet another person's learning, his artistic ability, his talent, and even his friendships. The truth remains—an unredeemed person is destined to covet regardless of whether he lives in Moscow or Paris, Washington or Hollywood. Covetousness knows no geographic barriers.

*Covetousness and its source.* Jesus did not denounce private property. He did not curse our desire to have food, shelter, clothes, and homes. Without these we cannot live. On the contrary, he praised and blessed those who provided for others their food and drink, their shelter, homes, clothes, and all things needful. Said he, "Blessed are you! I was thirsty and you gave me drink. I was hungry and you gave me meat . . . Enter into my Father's kingdom" (Matt. 25:35).

Talking about the rich man, Jesus deplored his blindness, his selfishness, his ethical, moral, and religious materialism. He was sorry for the man who knew nothing greater, nothing more precious than corn, wine, barns, possessions, and pleasure derived from them. He was sorry for the man who believed he was rich, yet knew neither the love of God nor the love of his fellow men. Basically, he was a poor man. His spiritual resources were as shallow as a puddle on a dirt road.

Today, as before, Christ would condemn the sin of our culture and the soil in which it has its roots. As before, he would condemn the advocates of selfish materialism and their slogans: "Just put your faith in the abundance of worldly goods; nothing can happen to us. Jut put your faith in our advanced technology; we will be able to produce everything. We will even create a perfect man. Just put your faith in our factories and barns and banks and missile strength, and all things will be added to you."

It is no good to have a multitude of everything stored up for this life and have nothing provided for one's eternal life. It is no good to have boats and cars and savings accounts without love and peace and truth and righteousness. It is no good to live in abundance produced by envy, greed, and selfish craving. They are sure to lead us to hell.

**Covetousness defeated.** The answer to covetousness is not in the abolition of property, government, or desire for progress and/or improvement. The answer to covetousness is not in the denial of a material world and its values. Neither asceticism (the torture of body, mind, and soul) nor a stylish "Lenten observance" could even begin to solve our problem.

A story is told about an old father whose son was awarded an Olympic crown. By his admirers, the young man was carried on their arms around the Olympic stadium. The old father stood nearby and clapped his hands, while tears were rolling over his cheeks. Another person, who stood close by, turned to the happy father and said, "It is time for you to die, for greater joy you will never know." His heart was filled with love. Covetousness was a million miles away.

The antidote to covetousness is love. Those whom we love, we cannot covet. Those for whom we pray, we cannot envy. Toward those who are dear to us, we cannot be jealous and greedy. We rejoice in their achievements, their victories, and their progress. By means of love, their happiness is our happiness. Their victory is our victory. Their joy is our joy.

*Conclusion:* Let us fight covetousness with koinonia.

Not with will alone but prayer also! Not with reason alone but emotional nature also! Not by ourselves alone but with God. Not in isolation but in an organic community.

## Our Christian Unity

*The Text:* "The glory which thou hast given me I have given to them, that they may be one even as we are one" (John 17:22).

*Introduction:* The New Delhi Conference.

Many positive things can be said about the New Delhi meeting which took place in November and December of 1961. It was a wonderful opportunity for Christian leaders from all over the world to come together, discuss their problems, and have fellowship with one another. It was an inspiration to see the Russian Orthodox Church, with its 50,000,000 communicants, being received into the membership of the World Council of Churches. Even the Church of Rome was sufficiently interested to send five official observers to this meeting.

Yet, some representatives were plagued by smallness. They could not overcome their liturgical barriers. They could not sit together at the Lord's table as God's family. From my point of view, this is more tragic than any words can say, for our deeds speak louder than our words.

*We speak of unity but practice separation.*   There are many good things we can say about the "ecumenical movement." Yet, again and again, my mind returns to the "ecumenical tragedy" of New Delhi. It seems to me that Professor Halford E. Luccock possessed almost prophetic powers when years ago he described the irony of the so-called "ecumenical movement" in a village setting.

"There was only one small drawback to this flourishing movement. All the time they kept working for disunity. In spite of the fervent praying, they all guarded, like a nervous bulldog, every denominational difference. Even on the most minute points of difference, scarcely visible to the naked eye of the bewildered townsmen, they took their stand like Martin Luther, saying 'Here I stand, I cannot do otherwise!' It is sad to relate that their small-minded and bigoted neighbors were more impressed by their actions for preserving disunity than by their ecstatic praise of unity. And so the good ship Ecumenical was becalmed in the doldrums."[15]

We talk big. We act small. We praise unity. We promote separation. No wonder we are called self-righteous hypocrites.

The alternatives are evident: either we give up the oratory and prayers for church unity, or do something really serious about church unity right now on the village level.

*Divisions are unnecessary, unworthy, deplorable and sinful.* In his book, *The Unfinished Reformation*, Dr. Charles Clayton Morrison expressed a conviction that sectarian denominationalism is exceedingly and scandalously wasteful of money, effort, and energy.[16] It seriously handicaps our missionary expansion.[17]

It is denominational sectarianism that frustrates our Christian social responsibilities. It robs us of our inherent strength in an inescapable competition with Roman Catholicism. No apology needs to be made. A competition exists.

It is denominational sectarianism which provincializes our mentality.

"No denomination can think in categories that are large enough to express the full range and majesty of the Christian faith. The denominational mind is necessarily narrow, provincial, short-sighted . . . It is an insult to Christian truth to build a sectarian wall around it."[18]

Denominationalism breeds a subtle and perilous moral insincerity. To quote Dr. Morrison again, "If any enlightened churchman will search his own heart, I believe he will find a conflict there between his sense of the hollowness and unreality of the claims of his denomination, on the one hand, and on the other hand, the practical necessity of supporting these claims in the interest of denominational morale."[19]

*We can make way to unity.* There are, of course, many obstacles and problems in the way yet to be overcome. Let us remember, ecumenicity does not require any theological uniformity whether it be conservative, liberal, fundamentalist or existentialist uniformity. Pertaining to profound religious, political, and theological issues, people are going to have different opinions until the very coming of the kingdom. However, in a genuine fellowship there is room enough for a variety of convictions and opinions and persuasions. Ecumenicity only requires tolerance, generosity of spirit, kindness, willingness to respect those who happen to have a different point of view. It requires determination to work and worship and serve together in love.

From my point of view, ecumenicity does not require a liturgical uniformity. There is nothing in the prayer of Jesus that says all Christians should worship absolutely in the same fashion; that all orders of worship should be the same; that all ministers should wear the same robes; that all church members should experience beauty or goodness or love in the same fashion. Ecumenicity only requires that we be generous, kind and respectful in regard to the feelings, convictions, and liturgical practices of others.

Ecumenicity does not require uniformity in church polity. No organization of polity principle is an infallible one. There are no sacrosanct principles of polity. The only ideas which are incongrous with the Protestant tradition are those of infallibility, intolerance, heresy hunting, religious dictatorship, and spiritual totalitarianism.

*Conclusion:* Ecumenicity is our goal.

The local church is true to the spirit of Christ only when it is ready to work for unity, co-operation, and inclusiveness. The local church is the "Body of Christ" only when it knows no segregation and discrimination, when it knows itself as an organic part of the whole church, when it recognizes responsibilities which transcend its independence and autonomy. To promote the spirit of ecumenicity is a sacred responsibility of you and me.

**CHAPTER EIGHT**

# TOWARD HEALTHY GROWTH And MATURITY

The preacher who has done his pastoral work is well aware that widespread are the problems of immaturity—oversensitivity, insecurity, impulsiveness, impatience, irresponsibility, self-centeredness. Such attitudes may be clearly detectable, or they may be hidden behind various masks. Whatever the situation, as preachers we have a profound responsibility to deal with such issues in our sermons. Our parishioners are eager to hear us preach on problems of (1) insecurity, (2) temptations, (3) unworthiness, (4) mature relationships, and (5) acceptance.

Following are outlines and excerpts of sermons preached with a view to promoting healthy growth and maturity.

## Security in an Insecure World

*The Text:* "And thou shalt be secure because there is hope . . . Yea, thou shalt take thy rest in safety . . . Thou shalt lie down, and none shall make thee afraid" (Job 11:18, 19 K.J.V.).

*Introduction:* We are living in an insecure world.

Our existence is threatened by poverty and disease, loss and depression, enemy bombs and missiles, sin and separation, finitude and death. This is a bitter conflict, and sometimes we become frantic about our insecurity. Not long ago our thoughts were turned to the building of bomb shelters. I do not want to make anyone feel guilty if he has undertaken such a project. If carried on as a community enterprise, without despair, panic, and illusion, it is as sane and sound an action as taking a shelter from natural disasters.

Yet, even the very best bomb shelters cannot provide sufficient security. It must come from deep within and high above.

*Sufficient security demands exposure.* Our insecurity is basically a matter of hiding. We feel insecure because we are afraid that some hidden secrets will come to light, that deep within us are "skeletons, hobgoblins—yes, dinosaurs, vultures, and pythons."[1] The truth is, these are a threat to our security only while we keep them from exposure.

Our insecurity is in separation. We feel insecure because we are separated from our true selves, from our inner rootage, from our inner powers, from the ground of our being. This kind of insecurity is not solved by shelters of steel, rock, and cement. There is no medicine, no tranquilizer, no wisdom, no virtue that can substitute for truthful self-confrontation, self-exposure, self-knowledge.

Our insecurity is a matter of hiding from God. He knows our dreams of omnipotence and childish illusions, our feelings of rebellion and guilt. Our security is in self-exposure: "Thou hast searched me and known me . . . Thou knowest when I sit down and when I rise up; thou discernest my thoughts from afar . . . Even before a word is on my tongue, lo, O Lord, thou knowest it altogether" (Psalm 139:1-2, 4).

*Security demands affirmation.* Hardships, troubles, and crises of life will remain until the end of days. Yet, inner resources to solve problems, to overcome obstacles, and to endure that which is beyond control will also remain until the end of days.

Ultimately, sufficient security does not depend upon what we have but what we are. H. E. Fosdick is right in saying, "No man is finally defeated until he thinks he is."[2]

To achieve sufficient security, therefore, we must be hard at work to liberate ourselves from the inner causes which disturb our serenity. We need to remind ourselves constantly that God is and he cares.

A little girl, with her parents, was on a German evacuation ship in the Baltic Sea. The ship was apparently torpedoed by a Russian sub. Orders came from the captain for passengers to put on their life belts. They were provided for all except little children. As the little girl watched her father put on his life belt, she said, "Daddy, why are you doing this?" The father answered, "This belt will help us float on the water in case the ship goes down." "But Daddy, I have no belt. When we are in the water, you'll hold me up, won't you, Daddy?" This was an expression of a confident trust, a childish trust indeed—yet, one we need today in order to live in sufficient security in an insecure world.

Basically, sufficient security depends upon our realization that it (security) is not the ultimate purpose of life.

**Security is born in adventure with God.** Confidence and trust in God are not born in an idleness of the soul. To paraphrase the words of Conrad Aiken, they are born in that voluntary decision to walk forward into the darkness without vision. They are born in that decision to handle this darkness with hands unready, yet brave.

Sufficient security is ours when we stand ready to give ourselves to a cause. A man who was determined to become a pilot had to conquer a multitude of hardships. First, he had to overcome his inefficiency in mathematics. He struggled hard and finally passed the test in math. His second obstacle was air sickness. Every time he flew his craft, he became terribly sick. It looked as if he would never make it. He prayed and said, "God, help me get over this fear. I know it is mind over matter." He succeeded. Then came an extraordinary test. The altitude was 30,000 feet. He was flying a very expensive Air Force bomber. As he prepared to descend, he discovered that his landing gear was out of order. He radioed the control tower. They advised, "Keep on flying until all gas is gone." This he did. The landing gear still did not work. Again he asked the control tower what to do. The officer said, "There are three things you can do. First, you may parachute over the ocean and let the plane go down into the sea, hoping that you will survive. Second, you may parachute over land and let your plane crash. Or, you may try a 'belly landing.'" He prayed again. Then he decided to make a "belly landing." It was an exciting moment for all. Fire trucks were ready. Spectators gathered. Everyone was breathless. He tried once, almost hitting the ground. He tried again. This time he made a perfect landing. Everybody shouted and applauded. A newsman asked, "How did you do it?" The answer came: "I put myself in the hands of God and let go. Everything worked out perfectly." *Conclusion:* Our greatest enemies: fear and selfish possessiveness.

Our opportunities to fight against these enemies are unlimited. The best of them is an opportunity to live and work for the security of others while we place ourselves in the hands of God.

Bishop Polk had come to visit a dying slave who had promised to give his life that someone else might live. When the final moment came, the Bishop said to the slave, "Are you all right or are you afraid?" The answer was brave and clear, "Should love be afraid of death or hesitant to give too much?" A wonderful security in an insecure world! You will rest in safety and none will make you afraid!

## When You Are Tempted

*The Text:* "Blessed is the man who endures trial, for when he has stood the test he will receive the crown of life which God has promised to those who love him" (James 1:12).

*Introduction:* All are subject to temptation.

The saints and the sinners, the mature and the immature, the young and the old, all are subject to temptations. For temptations are founded in the ethical-moral constitution of persons.[3] Blessed are those who can say "yes" to the potentialities of good and "no" to the potentialities of evil.

***Temptation of sensuous desire.*** For forty days Jesus had fasted in the wilderness. Most likely, he had done this to clarify the goals of his life, making sure he understood the spiritual values he wanted to realize. Now, having been forty days without food, he was hungry. Hardly a more powerful temptation could have come to him at this moment than the temptation to make the satisfaction of his sensuous needs the goal of his life. Yet, Christ was not blinded by his temptation. He saw the deceitfulness of his own hunger. The question is: Are we equally alert? To be sure, we must have bread to live. Shelter and clothes we must have also. Yet, we are not merely physical beings that live by food, shelter, clothes, and the satisfaction of our sensuous needs. We are living souls. We have our spiritual and our intellectual needs and demands. These we dare not deny.

Yet, there are moments when our sensuous desire seizes mastery over our life with irresistible power. "All at once, a secret, smouldering fire is kindled. The flesh burns and is in flames."[4] Where can we draw the power to overcome? Bonhoeffer is right: through the image of the Crucified. "Against this power the power of desire breaks up into nothingness. . . . Here I realize that the lust of the flesh is nothing else than the anguish of the flesh in the face of death."[5]

*Reliance on miracles.* Jesus knew that a belief in magic and miracles was common among his people. These they believed to be the infallible signs of God. The more miraculous, the more divine. What is absolutely impossible to men is possible to God. The area of God's activity is precisely this one: to break the laws he has established, and thus manifest his omnipotence. "Why not exploit this superstition and prove myself to be the Son of God?" was his thought.

Our Lord was not blinded by the lights of either magic, miracle, or superstition. His answer was clear and uncompromising. I will not ask the Lord my God to break the rational strucure of his universe! I will not pray for the performance of a miracle for the sake of self-glorification. I will not place myself above law, order, and common humanity!

It may be well to note, the irrational presupposition back of Christ's temptation does not belong to the past exclusively. We, too, may be tempted to live in an atmosphere of an illusion, tempted to imagine the world as it is not, tempted to wait for a miracle to do for us what we ought to do for ourselves. For numerous illustrations (and enjoyment) I suggest the reading of Halford E. Luccock's *Like a Mighty Army.*

The final appeal came through *the temptation of sovereignty.*

The tempter said to him, "You want authority, power, influence, and success. Behold, all this and more will be yours if only you will bow down before me and surrender. Deny now and then—not always—your ethical idealism, your notions of righteousness, honesty, truthfulness, humility, and non-violence. All this and more will be yours!"

The choice Jesus made we know. His purpose in life was not be the lord and master over others. He would not, even for a short moment, stoop to the level of flattery, dishonesty, revenge, and hate. His destiny was to love, serve, and bless.

The aspirations for power, authority, success, and temporal glory are as universal today as they were yesterday. They are bound to lure us all with words that may seem to reflect wisdom and common sense. "You don't have to be too honest, although honesty is the best policy. A little dishonesty won't hurt a bit. Just compromise.

Bow down before me for a little while and you will be King forever."

*Conclusion:* How does a Christian answer? He knows how to unmask the devil.

First, you cannot deceive God. You cannot escape consequences ever. Secondly, he knows God was with him. God is with him. God will be with him always. God's grace is sufficient.

### Beyond Improper Self-evaluation

*The Text:* "When I was a child, I spoke like a child, I thought like a child, I reasoned like a child; when I became a man, I gave up childish ways" (I Cor. 13:11).

*Introduction:* Our problem is improper self-esteem.

So often we are overwhelmed by feelings of unworthiness. We imagine that we have no resources to be creative. Even more, we live in an illusion that our feelings of inferiority cannot be overcome. In reality, these are childish feelings. They can be overcome.

**Think about biblical personalities.** When Moses was called to be a spokesman for God and a leader of his people, his answer was "No." As he looked at himself, he could find a host of reasons for his answer. He thought he could not speak. He felt guilty over what he had done in the past. He imagined others laughing at him. He knew he was aggressive, impatient, impulsive. He did not think that God could change him now that he was already a young man. Yet, the time came when Moses gave up childish feelings. He looked squarely in his own face. He made a positive decision. He accepted his responsibility. As a result, out of a handful of people, he created a nation that has not died and most likely will not die.

When Jeremiah was called to his prophetic mission he said, "Ah, Lord God! Behold, I do not know how to speak, for I am only a youth" (Jer. 1:6). He, too, felt inferior. He had all kinds of excuses. Yet God met all of his objections. Said he, "Do not say, 'I am only a youth'; for to all to whom I send you you shall go, and whatever I command you you shall speak. Be not afraid of them, for I am with you to deliver you" (Jer. 1:7, 8). Jeremiah accepted God's promise and became a forerunner of Jesus.

At the time they were called, many of the disciples of Jesus felt inferior and unworthy. There was Matthew, the tax collector. No decent Galilean would come to his house. No one would ever invite his wife or children for a visit. Lonely! Friendless! Despised! Cursed! Rejected! Afraid even to go to the temple. Ashamed even to look up in prayer. Yet, when Jesus called him, he followed. He accepted Jesus' promise (Luke 19:10; Matt. 9:13). He was changed.

There were many others. Simon the Zealot, full of hostility and aggressiveness. There was Peter, unstable, boastful, vacillating, impulsive, emotional. They, too, learned to understand themselves. As they retraced the steps of their experiences in the past, new light was shed upon their way. They began to look at life with hope. They learned to accept, forgive, and love. With Paul they could say, "When I was a child, I spoke like a child, I thought like a child, I reasoned like a child; when I became a man, I gave up childish ways."

**Retrace your development.** A well-known minister tells us that he had a very unfortunate beginning. He was the second child in his family. His older brother was far superior in almost every way. For years he kept on comparing himself with his brother. Any time he did it, he felt inferior. A complex developed and did its harmful work until the man learned to know and understand his emotional heritage.

There are many circumstances that often bring about injured feelings in children. These include alcoholism in the family, parental instability, an unhappy home situation, death of one or both parents, economic hardships and lack of religious orientation in the early home. In a multitude of situations also, guilt has played an important part.

To retrace our development is not always pleasant. Deep down in our souls we may feel inferior, unwanted, unloved and unimportant. Yet, we do not want to admit it even to ourselves. By "compensating," by "showing off," we may try to hide our true feelings from friends and foes alike. We may be whistling in the dark, hoping that this will make us brave. It is only a self-deception. There is no substitute for our innermost honesty.

**Behold your creative potentialities.** In every human being there are a multitude of creative potentialities. Even the blind, the deaf, and the lame are richly endowed. The sick, the sorrowing, and the suffering fellows of humanity are not forgotten by God. Many of them have far outshone their brothers deprived of human tragedy.

In his book, *On Being a Real Person*, Dr. Fosdick illustrates this point beyond a doubt. We do not need to remain the way we are. God is within us to change our aggressiveness into calm repose, our impatience into confident awaiting (Isa. 40:31), our perfectionistic reaching for the impossible into a realistic self-acceptance.

God is working within us to make us resolute and steadfast. He is ready to help us face and accept our responsibilities. We must begin where we are.

Miss G. is a commuter. She lives on Long Island and works in New York City. Her daily commutation time is two hours. I said to her, "What a waste of time." She replied, "Not at all. I manage to keep myself busy." When I asked her to explain, she told about the books she had read on the train. "And," she said, "most important of all—I keep on building an image of God constantly working within me. This image has changed the low estimate I used to have of myself. Now I am ready to accept my share of responsibilities."

**You belong to God.**   Not long ago I was talking to a man who thought that he was of no use in this world. He considerd himself a burden to others. I asked him, "Would a loving father ever think of his children as burdens?" Of course not! And God is our Father! Therefore, if God be for us, who can be against us? (Rom. 8:16, 17; I John 4:4; 3:24).

To triumph over our sense of unworthiness we need to understand that we are all God's children. He has created us in his own image (Genesis 1:27). He has given us of his own spirit (I John 3:24). He has sent Christ to be our Savior (John 3:16). His love includes us all. To him, there are no unwanted children, no worthless individuals!

God wants us to grow in love. No power in the world can expel from our hearts the feeling of supersensitivity, suspicion, and impatience as can the love of Christ. Says Paul, "Love is patient and kind; love is not jealous or boastful; it is not arrogant or rude. Love does not insist on its own way; it is not irritable or resentful; it does not rejoice at wrong, but rejoices in the right. Love bears all things, believes all things, hopes all things, endures all things. Love never ends" (I Cor. 13:4–8a).

*Conclusion:* With God, we are grown-up persons—in our thoughts, in our feelings, in our words, in our choices, in our responsibilities, in our goals and perspectives, in our relationships with ourselves and others.

### Honor Builds; Dishonor Destroys

*The Text:* "Honor your father and your mother, that your days may be long in the land which the Lord your God gives you" (Exodus 20:12).

*Introduction:* Problems of human relations begin early.

Joe was an only child. He had no brothers or sisters. He was the pride and joy of his mother. His father was stern, puritanical, demanding. Joe never learned to love and respect his father. Resentment developed early. It grew to such an extent that Joe's normal growth and development were hindered. Later in life, Joe had continuous troubles with his marriage partner, his supervisors, and his neighbors. More often than not, Joe was a headache also to his minister. Everything had to be his way. He had not learned to love and honor his parents.

***See with both eyes.*** Christ does not demand that we be blindly sentimental, unrealistic, dreamy. Some people are hard to understand, and much harder to love, honor, and respect. Catherine X. is a fine college student. She is conscientious, friendly, outgoing. Yet, she has a problem of loving and honoring her mother. "My mother is a stranger to me," says Catherine. "She never spent time with us children. We have never discussed any of the problems of life together. She has time for all kinds of activities. While she spends time in the theatrical fellowship, I have to clean the house, wash the dishes, wash the laundry, take care of my six brothers and sisters. My mother is a show-off. She does not speak the truth. She does not really believe what she pretends to believe. How can I love and honor her?"

It is easy to pass judgment on our parents. Yet, little do we know about their background. We do not know all about their burdens, sorrows, disappointments. These they do not wish to share with us simply for our protection. If Catherine knew "the whole story" she would have different feelings. In order to love and honor others, we have to learn to see with both eyes.

*Only cowards seek a scapegoat.* If you have been around long enough, you know how often people look for a scapegoat. Responsibility is hard to accept. And, the more immature we are, the less willing we are to face our life situation. The truth of the matter is that mature relationships depend upon shared responsibilities between parents and children, husbands and wives, employers and employees. Each of us needs to accept his fair share of responsibility.

A young couple, aged seventeen and eighteen, wanted to get married. Both were college students. They came for counsel and friendly guidance. I asked them about their future plans. Both were quick to say they had not thought about the future in any detail. As our conversation continued, it was evident they had not looked realistically at their life situation. Both were living in a dream world. I felt very sorry for them, for I have seen too many marriages start with sex drive and no responsibility.

Mature relationship involves understanding—seeing with both eyes. It also involves an acceptance of responsibility.

*Harmonize your drives.* Absolute independence in life is a childish dream. In numerous ways we depend upon others. As family members, Americans, human beings, we belong together. United we are strong. Divided we are weak. To paraphrase the words of the late President Kennedy, as long as we are united, there is nothing we cannot do. When we are divided, there is nothing we can do.

Each of us has the desire to belong. We have to respect and recognize this basic need if we are to have rootage and being. When we suppress it, we are uprooted and blown by the wind as bubbles of soap.

At the same time, we also want to be independent. Each of us has his own feelings, ambitions, expectations. The voice within says, "To your own self be true. Be independent! Make your own choice and stick to your decision." Thanks be to God that this is so. Without this, there is no authentic existence. Yet, as we can rely too much on others and hinder our growth by dependence, so also we can become rebellious, destructive, egotistic, in constant emphasis on independence.

Maturity means harmony and wholeness. The prodigal son learned this lesson the hard way. He suffered much. He wasted much of his precious life. We need not repeat his errors.

*Conclusion:* Honor builds; dishonor destroys.

Whether our heritage is large or small, the way to preserve it and enrich it is by using whatever is good, true, lovely, and praiseworthy as a foundation for building upon it a structure of lasting values.

A woman whose husband died when her children were very small worked desperately hard to give her sons the very best education available. When all three of them were established, Mrs. X. was at the end of her days. Before she died, her oldest son came to the hospital and whispered in her ear, "Mother, we love you so much." Mrs. X. opened her eyes and said, "My dear John, why didn't you say it before."

## The New Person in Christ

*The Text:* "If anyone is in Christ, he is a new creation" (II Cor. 5:17).

*Introduction:* What do we mean by "new creation."

"If I were asked to sum up the Christian message in two words," says Paul Tillich, "I would say with Paul: it is the message of a 'new creation.' "[6] With this we all would have to agree wholeheartedly. Yet, the question remains: "What do you mean by the new creation, by the new person in Christ?"

The new man in Christ is not callous, insensitive, or especially protected. He is destined to have his share of troubles and hardships, of pain, sorrow, and suffering.

The new man in Christ is not—and he cannot be—perfect in holiness, in love and purity. As all of us, he too falls short of the glory and the goodness and the beauty of God.

The new man in Christ is not—and cannot be—100 percent successful in everything. He, too, is destined to have his share of failures and disappointments. He may be troubled on every side. In some ways he may appear to be the same old grouch. And yet, paradoxically enough, if he is in Christ, he is a new creation. One thing can certainly be said about him: By perplexing troubles and problems *he is not driven to despair.*

The new man in Christ does not know the answers to all of the problems of the world. He knows that his knowledge is limited. A very large shadow of mystery covers the earth. He is aware that there is a form of suffering and pain in this world which does not seem to do any good to anyone. He is puzzled, as we are, about the existence of incurable mental and physical ailments and disorders. He is perplexed by unbearable pain and suffering which often impose themselves upon human beings. He is troubled by the fact that people inherit ailments and sometimes limited powers of comprehension. Yet, he is not frightened into looking for an escape.

The new man in Christ is perplexed by the victories that appear to be evil. Natural disasters baffle him. He is aware that he, too, may be forced into the "valley of the shadows" where we are destined to pray, "My God, my God" (Matt. 27:46). Yet, he is free from living in fearful anticipation.

The new man in Christ knows that he has no final explanation about either the beginning or the end of all things. He knows he cannot comprehend all mysteries of life, of his own existence, much less the mysteries of God's timeless and endless universe. Yet, by the dark unknown, he is not frightened into deadly depression.

The new man in Christ is not driven to despair because he is reconciled with existence, with nature, with destiny, with God himself. And this has come about not so much through good deeds, good prayers, good rituals and ways of appeasement. For God needs none of these in order to accept us. He has accepted us all as we are. All we need it to accept His acceptance.

A medical doctor was driven to despair. His was a heartbreaking story. Said he, "My father and my mother rejected me. They beat me so I could not sit for months. You will not believe this, but I had to eat with the cows. I was rejected. No one believes me. Do you?" My answer followed. "Surely, I do. Your feeling is real. Your soul was injured early in life. The injury was never overcome. What you are saying means painful memories—some fact, some interpretation, some preservation of childhood imagination. It has been triggered now by another feeling of rejection. I understand you. In a labor camp in Germany I felt I was rejected even by God. I prayed, 'My God, my God, why has thou forsaken me?'

And then I learned the truth. You are never rejected by God. He accepts you. He loves you. He wants you to draw near and believe!"

Even more, the new man in Christ may be afflicted in many ways, yet *he is not crushed by his afflictions.*

On the road of God's service, there is no impasse. We may be harried, yet never are we hemmed in. God never refuses to help.

According to the testimony of faith, when the Israelites were oppressed in Egypt, suffering mental and physical agony, pain and humiliation, God provided an open door. When the same Israelites were hungering and thirsting in the desert, tired birds came into their reach and honey dew was made available to them for manna. Neither were they forsaken when the time came to cross the great river. The new man in Christ is not crushed by his afflictions because he knows that God's resources will always be available.

The new man in Christ may be destined to experience shipwrecks, beatings, trials, tribulations, loneliness, a "thorn in the flesh," nakedness, famine, peril, and sword. Yet, he is destined to remain steadfast and uncrushed because he knows that failures, deficiencies and afflictions need not be taken as a curse. They can be immensely valuable, helpful, and stimulating. And when accepted, they become great assets in life.

As Carl Rogers has pointed out, El Greco must have realized that real artists do not paint "like that." Yet, he kept on painting as if to say, "Great artists do not paint like that, but I do!"[7] Or to move to another area, Ernest Hemingway must have said to himself, "Great writers do not write like that, but I do." Or, to take such a genius as Albert Einstein, he too may have known that academically trained physicists do not think like that. Yet, he kept on thinking like that, as if to say, "They do not, but I do!" Through their courage, the world has been blessed in a marvelous way.

The new man in Christ is not crushed by his afflictions because he accepts them and bravely looks at his innermost feelings, even his inner fears, his loneliness, his self-pity, his hidden resentments and hostilities. He is not crushed because "he accepts himself as something which is eternally important, eternally loved, eternally accepted, eternally precious."[8]

And so, as he thus accepts the free-flowing grace and acceptance of God, as he accepts himself, he becomes rooted, grounded, and anchored in Christ, the new life: new power, new vitality, new energy, new enthusiasms, new confidence, new trust, new spirit. Christ is all of these.

***He has an outgoing purpose.*** Our need for self-preservation is very common. It may be regarded a part of the old order. Yet, I am not ready to identify it exclusively with the old order. Not everything about self-preservation is negative. There is much we must keep and preserve—our health, strength, and energy.

All of us have to watch out for our well-being. Under given circumstances, if we do not, no one else will. Self-affirmation is positive.[9]

Yet, the life of a new person in Christ is not—and cannot be—centered in either self-preservation, self-protection, self-security, or self-salvation. It must have a larger purpose: a dedication to extend a hand, to give a lift, to build a dream, to manifest love and appreciation to others.

In many ways, as T. P. Ferris has put it, Jesus was very strange. He gave up his job to undertake a mission without pay. That mission was a failure. Yet, he himself was the most successful man among us all.[10]

He had no worldly security. Yet, he was so secure that he could stoop and wash the feet of his disciples. He went to dine with his people not because he wanted a contract, but because he wanted to give them the new life, the power to transcend the old creation.[11]

*Conclusion:* New life in Christ awaits us all.

We only need to let the old life go. It is worthless currency! We only need to turn to God with the words of him who said, "I will arise and go to my father . . ." (Luke 15:18a). God will fulfill his promise. He will grant us new life.

# NOTES

## CHAPTER ONE

1. See Russell L. Dicks, *My Faith Looks Up* (Philadelphia: The Westminster Press, 1959), p. 75.
2. Franklin H. Littell, Ed., *Sermons to Intellectuals* (New York: The Macmillan Company, 1963), pp. vii, viii.
3. Dietrich Bonhoeffer, *The Cost of Discipleship* (New York: The Macmillan Company, 1948), p. 37ff.
4. H. E. Fosdick, *A Book of Public Prayers* (New York: Harper & Row, Publishers, 1959), p. 116.
5. James W. Clarke, *Dynamic Preaching* (Westwood, N.J.: Fleming H. Revell Company, 1960), p. 65.
6. C. H. Dodd, *The Apostolic Preaching and Its Development* (New York: Harper & Row, Publishers, 1936).
7. Paul Rowntree Clifford, *The Pastoral Calling* (Great Neck, N.Y.: Channel Press, 1961), p. 59.
8. Roy Pearson, *The Ministry of Preaching* (New York: Harper & Row, Publishers, 1959), p. 17.
9. Donald G. Miller, *Fire in Thy Mouth* (Nashville: Abingdon Press, 1954), pp. 17, 122.
10. James W. Clarke, *op. cit.*, p. 68.
11. *Ibid.*, p. 68.
12. Edgar N. Jackson, *A Psychology for Preaching* (Great Neck, N.Y.: Channel Press, 1961), p. 75.
13. Gene E. Bartlett, *The Audacity of Preaching* (New York: Harper & Row, Publishers, 1962), p. 43.

## CHAPTER TWO

1. Paul Rowntree Clifford, *op. cit.*, p. 73.
2. Richard C. Cabot and Russell L. Dicks, *The Art of Ministering to the Sick* (New York: The Macmillan Company, 1936), pp. 13–15.
3. Paul Tillich, *The New Being* (New York: Charles Scribner's Sons, 1955), pp. 20, 25.
4. Phillips Brooks, *Lectures on Preaching* (London: Allenson, 1895), p. 255.

5. Seward Hiltner, "Pastoral Counseling and the Ministry," from *Making the Ministry Relevant,* Hans Hofmann, Ed. (New York: Charles Scribner's Sons, 1960), p. 128.
6. *Ibid.,* p. 128.
7. Edgar Jackson, *op. cit.,* p. 158.

### Chapter Three

1. (New York: Bantam Books, 1960), p. 16.
2. *Ibid.,* p. 17.
3. (New York: Liveright Publishing Corporation, 1949), p. 86.
4. S. R. Slavson, *An Introduction to Group Therapy* (New York: International Universities Press, 1954).
5. Edgar Jackson, *op. cit.,* p. 121.
6. Reuel L. Howe, *The Miracle of Dialogue* (New York: The Seabury Press Incorporated, 1963), p. 3.
7. *Ibid.*
8. Earl H. Ferguson, "Abstractions in Preaching," *Pastoral Psychology,* Vol. 14, No. 137 (October, 1963), p. 8.
9. *Op. cit.,* p. 15.
10. *Op. cit.,* p. 53.
11. Harry Emerson Fosdick, *Riverside Sermons* (New York: Harper & Row, Publishers, 1958), pp. 46, 54, 63, 83, 94, 122.
12. *Op. cit.,* p. 95.
13. Roy Pearson, *op. cit.,* p. 94.

### Chapter Four

1. Paul Tournier, *A Doctor's Casebook in the Light of the Bible* (New York: Harper & Row, Publishers, 1960), pp. 162–168.
2. *Ibid.,* pp. 164, 165.
3. Emily Gardiner Neal, *God Can Heal You Now* (Englewood Cliffs, N.J.: Prentice-Hall, Inc., 1958).
4. Jane Huff, *Whom the Lord Loveth* (New York: McGraw-Hill Book Co., Inc., 1961).
5. Leslie D. Weatherhead, *Psychology, Religion and Healing* (New York: Abingdon-Cokesbury Press, 1951).
6. Paul Tournier, *op. cit.,* pp. 169–177.
7. Emily Gardiner Neal, *op. cit.,* p. 121.
8. Smiley Blanton, M.D., *Love or Perish* (New York: Simon & Schuster, 1956), p. 29.
9. Charles Morris, *The Open Self* (Englewood Cliffs, N.J.: Prentice-Hall, Inc., 1942), pp. 96–115.
10. (New York: The Macmillan Company, 1959).
11. (New York: Harper & Row, Publishers, 1960), p. 38.
12. Earl A. Loomis, Jr., M.D., *The Self in Pilgrimage* (New York:

Harper & Row, Publishers, 1960), pp. 81–93. Reprinted by permission of Ann Elmo Agency, Inc.

13. Karen Horney, M.D., *Self-Analysis* (New York: W. W. Norton & Co., Inc., 1942), p. 10.
14. See Vance Packard, *Hidden Persuaders* (New York: David McKay Co., 1957).
15. Victor Frankl, *Man's Search for Meaning* (Boston: Beacon Press, 1962).
16. Anton T. Boisen, *Out of the Depths* (New York: Harper & Row, Publishers, 1960).
17. James B. Ashbrook, "The Great God Bacchus" (Valley Forge, Pa.: Division of Christian Social Concern, American Baptist Convention).
18. Robert S. de Ropp, *Drugs and the Mind* (New York: St. Martin's Press, 1957).
19. Robert S. de Ropp, *op. cit.*
20. Smiley Blanton, *op. cit.*, p. 71.
21. Erich Fromm, *The Art of Loving* (New York: Harper & Row, Publishers, 1956).
22. Frederick Kates, *The Use of Life* (New York: Harper & Row, Publishers, 1953), p. 84.
23. Elton Trueblood, *The Humor of Christ* (New York: Harper & Row, Publishers, 1964).
24. O. S. Marden, *Architects of Faith* (New York: The Success Co., 1900), p. 101.
25. Tomi Keitlen with Norman M. Lobsenz, *Farewell to Fear* (New York: The Hearst Corporation, 1960).
26. (New York: Harper & Row, Publishers, 1956).
27. Edgar N. Jackson, *For the Living* (Des Moines: Channel Press, 1963), p. 29.
28. (New York: Simon & Schuster, Inc., 1946).
29. Catherine Marshall, *To Live Again* (Carmel, N.Y.: Guideposts Associates, Inc.).

## CHAPTER FIVE

1. Frank C. Laubach, *Channels of Spiritual Power* (Westwood, N.J.: Fleming H. Revell Company, 1954), p. 55.
2. For detailed study of anxiety see Milton R. Sapirstein's *Emotional Security* (New York: Crown Publishers, 1948), pp. 3–83.
3. James A. Pike, *The Next Day* (Garden City, N.Y.: Doubleday & Company, Inc., 1957).
4. Frank C. Laubach, *op. cit.*, p. 60.
5. (New York: Harper & Row, Publishers, 1955), p. 170.
6. Paul Tournier, *Escape from Loneliness,* translated by John S. Gilmour (Philadelphia: The Westminster Press, 1962).

7. Earl A. Loomis, Jr., *op. cit.,* p. 6.
8. Martin Buber, *I and Thou* (New York: Charles Scribner's Sons, 1958).
9. See Earl A. Loomis, Jr., *op. cit.,* p. 58.
10. W. L. Northridge, *Disorders of the Emotional and Spiritual Life* (Great Neck, N.Y.: Channel Press, 1961), p. 123.
11. Karl Menninger, M.D., *Love Against Hate* (New York: Harcourt, Brace and Company, 1942).
12. W. L. Northridge, *op. cit.,* p. 53.
13. Paul Tillich, *Systematic Theology* (Chicago: The University of Chicago Press, Vol. II, 1957), p. 68.
14. (New York: Longmans, Green & Co., The Gifford Lectures delivered at the University of Glasgow, 1935–37), p. 211.

## CHAPTER SIX

1. See Amos N. Wilder, *New Testament Faith for Today* (New York: Harper & Row, Publishers, 1955).
2. For discussion see "Myth, Symbol and Analogy" by Gustave Weigel, S. J., and "Christian Root-Terms: Kerygma, Mysterium, Kairos, Oikonomia" by Erich Przywara, S. J.; *Religion and Culture,* Walter Leibrecht, Ed. (New York: Harper & Row, Publishers, 1959).
3. Paul Tillich, *Systematic Theology, Vol. I* (Chicago: University of Chicago Press, 1951), p. 242.
4. See "The Predicament of the Christian Historian" by George Florovsky, *Religion and Culture,* Walter Leibrecht, Ed., pp. 144–167.
5. *The Pilgrim Hymnal* (Boston, Chicago: The Pilgrim Press, 1935), p. xxxvi.
6. Werner Keller, *Bible as History* (New York: William Morrow and Co., 1956).
7. *Revelation and Reason* (Philadelphia: The Westminster Press, 1956), p. 279.
8. Rudolf Bultmann, "New Testament and Mythology," *Kerygma and Myth, A Theological Debate,* Hans Werner Bartsch, Ed. (London: S.P.C.K., 1953), p. 1ff.
9. William Neil, *Modern Man Looks at the Bible* (New York: Association Press, 1958), p. 10.
10. *Christianity and History* (New York: Charles Scribner's Sons, 1950), p. 60.
11. Paul Tillich, *op. cit.,* p. 116.
12. Paul Johnson, *Psychology of Religion* (Nashville: Abingdon Press, 1959), p. 157.
13. *The Modern Use of the Bible* (New York: The Macmillan Company, 1944), p. 164.
14. St. Augustine, *Confessions X, xxviii.*

15. *The Pilgrim Hymnal, op. cit.,* hymn no. 233.
16. Willard L. Sperry, *Sermons Preached at Harvard* (New York: Harper & Row, Publishers, 1953), p. 108.
17. Charles R. Joy, Ed., *Albert Schweitzer, An Anthology* (Boston: The Beacon Press, 1947), p. 274.
18. Chad Walsh, *Behold the Glory* (New York: Harper & Row, Publishers, 1956), pp. 47–48.
19. Lucien Rudaux and G. De Vancouleurs, *Larousse Encyclopedia of Astronomy* (New York: Prometheus Press, 1959), p. 499.
20. Lois Phelps Johnson, *I'm Gonna Fly* (St. Paul, Minn.: Macalester Park Publishing Co., 1959).
21. From the pamphlet, *The Meaning of Hell,* published by Whittemore Associates, Inc., Boston, Mass.
22. Malcolm Boyd, *If I Go Down to Hell* (New York: Morehouse-Barlow Co., 1962), pp. 23–39.
23. Ashley Montague, *Immortality* (New York: Grove Press, 1955), p. 20.
24. *Ibid.,* p. 63.
25. Ivan Welty, *Through All the Seasons* (Westwood, N.J.: Fleming H. Revell Company, 1942), pp. 56–60.

CHAPTER SEVEN

1. Merrimon Cuninggim, *Freedom's Holy Light* (New York: Harper & Row, Publishers, 1955), p. 21.
2. Stuart Gerry Brown, Comp., *We Hold These Truths* (New York: Harper & Row, Publishers, 1941), p. 339.
3. John C. Bennett, *Christianity and Communism* (New York: Association Press, 1948), p. 9.
4. Karl Marx, *Das Kapital* (New York: The Modern Library, Inc., Random House, 1932), p. 341.
5. *Ibid.,* p. 335.
6. *Ibid.,* p. 340.
7. J. Edgar Hoover, *Masters of Deceit* (New York: Henry Holt & Co., 1958), p. 215.
8. Karl Marx, *op. cit.,* p. 355.
9. Herman Reissig, "How to Combat Communism" (New York: Council for Christian Social Action, United Church of Christ, 1961), p. 18.
10. Bruce Kenrick, *Come Out the Wilderness* (New York: Harper & Row, Publishers, 1962, and London: Collins, Publishers, 1962), p. 218.
11. John F. Kennedy, *Strategy for Peace* (New York: Harper & Row, Publishers, 1961), p. 208.
12. Karl Marx, *op. cit.,* p. 707.
13. *Ibid.,* p. 784.

14. See D. J. Dallin, *The Real Soviet Russia*, p. 189.
15. Halford E. Luccock, *Like a Mighty Army* (New York: Oxford University Press, 1954), p. 82.
16. Charles Clayton Morrison, *The Unfinished Reformation* (New York: Harper & Row, Publishers, 1953), p. 28ff.
17. *Ibid.*, pp. 32, 33.
18. *Ibid.*, p. 41.
19. *Ibid.*, p. 43.

## Chapter Eight

1. Earl A. Loomis, Jr., *op. cit.*, p. 5.
2. *The Power to See It Through* (New York: Harper & Row, Publishers, 1935), p. 40.
3. George S. Painter, *The Philosophy of Christ's Temptation* (Boston: Sherman, French & Company, 1914), p. 154.
4. Dietrich Bonhoeffer, *Temptation* (New York: The Macmillan Company, 1956), p. 33.
5. *Ibid.*, p. 34.
6. *The New Being* (New York: Charles Scribner's Sons, 1955), p. 15.
7. *On Becoming a Person* (Cambridge, Mass.: The Riverside Press, 1961), p. 175.
8. Paul Tillich, *op. cit.*, p. 22.
9. Erich Fromm, *Man For Himself* (New York: Holt, Rinehart and Winston, 1961), p. 130.
10. Theodore Parker Ferris, *The New Life in Christ* (Greenwich, Conn.: The Seabury Press, 1961), p. 24.
11. *Ibid.*, pp. 24–26.

# INDEX